Antiquity and Modernity

Classical Receptions

Series Editor: Maria Wyke, University College London

The ancient world did not end with the sack of Rome in the fifth century AD. Its literature, politics, and culture have been adopted, contested, used and abused, from the middle ages to the present day, by both individuals and states. The Classical Receptions Series presents new contributions by leading scholars to the investigation of how the ancient world continues to shape our own.

Antiquity and Modernity

Neville Morley

WILEY-BLACKWELL

A John Wiley & Sons, Ltd., Publication

This edition first published 2009
© 2009 by Neville Morley

Blackwell Publishing was acquired by John Wiley & Sons in February 2007.
Blackwell's publishing program has been merged with Wiley's global
Scientific, Technical, and Medical business to form Wiley-Blackwell.

Registered Office
John Wiley & Sons Ltd, The Atrium, Southern Gate, Chichester,
West Sussex, PO19 8SQ, United Kingdom

Editorial Offices
350 Main Street, Malden, MA 02148-5020, USA
9600 Garsington Road, Oxford, OX4 2DQ, UK
The Atrium, Southern Gate, Chichester, West Sussex, PO19 8SQ, UK

For details of our global editorial offices, for customer services, and for
information about how to apply for permission to reuse the copyright material
in this book please see our website at www.wiley.com/wiley-blackwell.

The right of Neville Morley to be identified as the author of this work has
been asserted in accordance with the Copyright, Designs and Patents Act 1988.

Wiley also publishes its books in a variety of electronic formats. Some content that
appears in print may not be available in electronic books.

Designations used by companies to distinguish their products are often claimed as
trademarks. All brand names and product names used in this book are trade names,
service marks, trademarks or registered trademarks of their respective owners. The
publisher is not associated with any product or vendor mentioned in this book. This
publication is designed to provide accurate and authoritative information in regard to
the subject matter covered. It is sold on the understanding that the publisher is not
engaged in rendering professional services. If professional advice or other expert
assistance is required, the services of a competent professional should be sought.

Library of Congress Cataloging-in-Publication Data

Morley, Neville.
Antiquity and modernity / Neville Morley.
p. cm. – (Classical receptions)
Includes bibliographical references and indexes.
ISBN 978-1-4051-3139-1 (hardcover : alk. paper)
1. Social science–Philosophy. 2. Social evolution.
3. History, Ancient–Philosophy. I. Title.

H61.15.M675 2008
300.1–dc22

2008010444

A catalogue record for this title is available from the British Library.

Set in 10/13pt Galliard
by Graphicraft Limited, Hong Kong
Printed and bound in Singapore
by Markono Print Media Pte Ltd

1   2009

For Anne

Eine Welt zwar bist du, o Rom; doch ohne die Liebe
Wäre die Welt nicht die Welt, wäre denn Rom auch nicht Rom.

Goethe, *Römische Elegien* I

Contents

Preface

From the end of the eighteenth century, commentators on human affairs became increasingly convinced that they and their society were experiencing an entirely new form of existence, which came to be labelled "modernity." The adjective "modern" had hitherto been synonymous with "contemporary," such that "modern art" was simply the art currently being produced in contrast to the art of the past, but increasingly "modern" came to imply a qualitative as well as a temporal distinction. Indeed, it became possible both to argue that some aspects of classical antiquity could be considered "modern," because of their resemblance to contemporary experience, and to assert that many parts of the modern world (largely, but not exclusively, areas outside Europe) were not, by any definition, "modern." Further, modernity came to be experienced as all-pervasive; all aspects of contemporary life and all the products of human endeavor were felt to embody and reflect this distinctive quality, to reveal the *Zeitgeist*, the spirit of the age.

This sense that life in the present was somehow quite different from the lives of previous generations gave new impetus to the investigation and analysis of human society and human nature; it resulted in new theories and ideas, and in entirely new fields of knowledge – the origins of disciplines like economics and sociology. To some extent this intellectual activity ran in parallel with, and was frequently inspired by, the rational investigation of the physical and natural worlds according to scientific methods rather than the received wisdom of scripture or the ideas inherited from the ancients. However, where the scientists and philosophers were dedicated to uncovering the universal and eternal principles that lay beneath the apparent confusion and variety of natural phenomena, the students of human behavior, social organization, and culture sought rather to strike a balance between the universal and the contingent. Most of them were concerned above all to understand their own society, not simply as an end in itself but in order to further its progress or address its deficiencies; they sought to identify universal principles in the apparent chaos of human history above all in order to understand the origins, nature, and dynamics of their own age.

Indeed, the sheer variety of political systems, social structures, forms of economic behavior, cultural activities, and even emotions and values across human history led many of these commentators to emphasize historical discontinuity far above continuity. The present was clearly distinguished from the past; modernity was entirely different from any previous form of human existence. In the course of the nineteenth century, the "sciences of modernity," sociology, political theory, psychology, and above all, economics, turned away from history; if they looked to the past at all, it was to those relatively recent periods which could plausibly be labeled as "proto-modern" and claimed as the starting point of the transformation of the world into its present state. Today, over a century later, this sense of the irrelevance of the past to the present persists, and, even when that is questioned, the idea of "modernity" is not; it is taken for granted that, despite all their manifest differences, the present and the early nineteenth century have something in common that distinguishes them from the rest of human history. Closer enquiry into what this commonality might be yields a bewildering range of theories and assertions, as each discipline – not to mention many individual thinkers – has developed at least one distinct interpretation of the nature of modernity. Somehow this incoherence does not matter; we remain firmly of the opinion that we are modern, and this denotes above all a separation from the past.

It seems remarkable that this taken-for-granted concept of modernity, and the many different (and often mutually contradictory) theories that have been developed to explain what may, after all, be an entirely imaginary object, have not been subjected to greater critical scrutiny. The reason may lie in the overwhelming scale of the task, since in principle almost every piece of writing from the late eighteenth century to the present could be taken as relevant to the history of the understanding of contemporary society as "modern." The aim of this book is more modest, though still daunting and overambitious: to approach this topic by considering the theme of the relation between "modernity" and the – arguably, equally taken-for-granted and equally imaginary – idea of "antiquity." The indifference to history found in later exponents of economics or sociology was not shared by the writers whose work laid the foundations for those new disciplines; on the contrary, their interpretations of the present, and indeed their sense that contemporary existence had a distinctive quality that needed to be identified and explained, were founded on constant reference to the past, and above all the classical past. Modernity was defined through contrast with different aspects of the past; its progress was measured against the yardstick of the greatest civilizations in history; ancient thinkers, while now clearly redundant in the interpretation of contemporary society, could still be important for understanding the dynamics of historical change that had eventually given rise to modernity. The past might even hold clues to the future, suggesting the eventual fate of even the most powerful civilizations, unless modernity could somehow break free of the inexorable processes of history. Even more importantly, for those writers who were less persuaded that modernity had surpassed all previous historical societies, the classical past offered a basis for criticism, a point of comparison that was not wholly in modernity's favor, and a vision of possible alternatives to the present state of things.

Modernity was defined and delineated by innumerable comparisons and contrasts between past and present, in many different texts, over the course of more than a century. Some writers developed such arguments explicitly and at length; others made only passing reference. Just as most texts from this period could be read as commenting in some way upon "modernity," so it is difficult to find an author who does not at some point offer a classical comparison or allusion; the influence of the literature and history of Greece and Rome was pervasive, and the influence of more general, non-specialist conceptions of "antiquity" was more pervasive still. A complete account of the confrontation of antiquity and modernity is clearly an impossible task; but, rather than concentrate solely on writers like Marx and Nietzsche, who comment extensively on the relation between ancient and modern, I have sought to draw in a wider range of authors and texts by organizing the material around themes. The selection has been driven partly by my sense of which writers in different disciplines have played the most important roles in the development of ideas of modernity – inevitably a subjective decision, in the absence of a comprehensive history of the concept – and partly by my judgment of which writers have the most interesting things to say on specific topics. I have little doubt that my selection, and the relative weight given to different texts and authors, will be a significant point of criticism, and my only defense is that I seek to identify themes and raise questions of potential significance rather than to offer a definitive account.

The other obvious objection is that, as an ancient historian, I am inclined to place far too much weight on passing references and commonplace allusions which simply reflect the dominance of the classics in eighteenth- and nineteenth-century education, rather than making any coherent attempt at conceptualizing modernity. This is of course possible, and may at any rate serve as a counterweight to the tendency of some modern commentators to ignore the classical references altogether. I do not claim that any but a few of these writers deliberately sets out to delineate modernity through the contrast with antiquity. Rather, they make such comparisons quite naturally and casually in the course of their discussions; these references may be taken, at the very least, as revealing their conceptions and assumptions, and so used as a way into the debate. However, I think they also reveal something else. The conviction that modernity exists and that we inhabit it, a conviction which above all expresses a sense of our location within and relation to history, was not the creation of any individual writer but is the effect of a continuing discourse, which is both reflected in these fragments and allusions and also, in part, constituted by them. They reveal a pervasive habit of drawing comparisons between ancient and modern and of understanding the present in terms of its difference from the past. Classical antiquity was chosen for the comparison above all because it was familiar; it is an open question as to whether another piece of the past might have served the same purpose, or whether the particular nature of classical antiquity as it was known and imagined – the blend of similarity and difference, or perhaps its susceptibility to being reimagined in the light of the present – made it especially suitable.

My interest in the place of the writings of Marx and Weber in the history of antiquity, and vice versa, predates my arrival at the University of Bristol, but it does not seem especially likely that this interest would have led to anything resembling this book if it had been left to its own devices in a less hospitable environment. Over the last decade I have enjoyed innumerable conversations and arguments about issues of reception and the classical tradition with colleagues like Catharine Edwards, Katherine Harloe, Duncan Kennedy, Aleka Lianeri, Charles Martindale, and Liz Potter; I have had the opportunity, with minimal effort, to encounter visiting scholars like Will Batstone, Jim Porter, Pierre Vidal-Naquet, and Hayden White, and to attend conferences and seminars on such themes as "Decadence Ancient and Modern" and "The Uses of

Reception"; I have had the immense pleasure of working in a department where exploring the relationship between ancient and modern and drawing on modern critical theory (and without any dogmatism as regards the choice of theoretical perspective) is regarded as entirely normal and unremarkable. All this has not only helped me to extend, develop, and refine my original interests, but given me the confidence to make them the focus of a study rather than just footnotes in more conventional historical work. Above all, I should like to thank Vanda Zajko, with whom over several years I taught a unit on "Antiquity and Modernity," exploring classical influences on Marx, Nietzsche, and Freud; besides the fact that this was one of the most stimulating and enjoyable teaching experiences of my career so far, many of the key ideas and arguments in this work were first developed in discussions and debates both in and about those classes.

This is a book built on other books. My role has, at times, felt less like that of a writer of history – a comprehensive account of the development of the idea of "modernity" and its relation to "antiquity" within different national and disciplinary traditions is far beyond the scope of this work – than like that of the organizer and chair of a large international conference. I have selected the subject and the contributors, and within certain limits have the power to decide how topics should be addressed and who should address them. I can ask, say, Schiller to respond to Weber, and can try to encourage the more eminent contributors to address specific questions rather simply reiterating their familiar positions; all this in the hope that the event will amount to more than the sum of its parts, and that new ideas and perspectives will emerge from the record of discussion. I would therefore like to acknowledge those whose ideas have particularly helped, in different ways, to inspire this gathering of distinguished thinkers: Marcel Berman's *All That Is Solid Melts Into Air*; David Harvey's *The Condition of Postmodernity*; Reinhard Koselleck's *Futures Past*; the works of George E. McCarthy on classical influences in nineteenth- and twentieth century German thought; James I. Porter's *Nietzsche and the Philology of the Future*; Bernard Yack's *The Longing for Total Revolution*. These books, along with the Bristol Classics Department, constitute a context that made this work possible.

Naturally I also have more practical debts: to seminar and conference audiences in Berlin, Bristol, Cambridge, Copenhagen, Glasgow, Manchester, and St Andrews, who commented on earlier versions of some of these ideas; to Alfred Bertrand at Blackwell and the readers of the original book proposal, for their exceptionally constructive and helpful comments and suggestions; to friends and colleagues like Gillian Clark and Bob Fowler, for continuing support and encouragement; to Angharad, whose conversation can be counted upon to illuminate and enliven; and, as ever, to Anne, for all her support, understanding and patience.

Note on References

For ease of reading, the various eighteenth- and nineteenth-century writings which are the subject of this study are referred to in the notes using the "short title" system, and listed in the Bibliography of Sources; references to modern works are given according to the Harvard "author–date" system.

Par ce qui c'est fait considérons ce qui se peut faire.

Through what has been done, let us consider what can be done.
Jean-Jacques Rousseau, *Of the Social Contract*

Denn ich wüsste nicht, was die classicher Philologie in unserer
Zeit für einen Sinn hätte, wenn nicht den, in ihr unzeitgemäss – das
heist gegen die Zeit und dadurch auf die Zeit und hoffentlich zu
Gunsten einer kommenden Zeit – zu wirken.

For I do not know what meaning classical studies would have in
our time if not that of working in their untimeliness – that is to say,
against our time and thereby on our time and, let us hope, for the
benefit of a time to come.
Friedrich Nietzsche, "On the uses and disadvantages
of history for life"

1

Untimely Knowledge

Antonio Gramsci, the twentieth-century Italian communist theoretician, may seem an unlikely defender of the benefits of a classical education. Nevertheless, like many radical thinkers of the previous century, he had followed a traditional curriculum in school and university, specializing in Latin and Greek grammar as well as linguistics and geography; like them, he drew from this education some surprising conclusions, using it as a basis for thinking about different aspects of contemporary society.[1] In late 1930, four years into his imprisonment under Mussolini, he turned his thoughts to the subject of the Fascist reform of the Italian educational system:

> Schools were thus divided into classical and technical (vocational but not manual) schools, which called into question the very principle of the pursuit of general culture, of a humanistic orientation, of a general culture based on the classical tradition. This pursuit, once questioned, can be said to be destroyed, since its formative capacity was largely based on the general prestige enjoyed by a particular form of civilization. The tendency today is to abolish every type of school that is "disinterested" (in other words, not motivated by immediate interests) and "formative," or else to leave only a scaled-down specimen of such a school for a tiny elite of rich persons and young ladies who need not bother with preparing themselves for the future.[2]

In the old school, then, the organizational structure itself provided an education. How? The study of Latin and Greek and other languages, together with the study of their respective literatures and political histories, was at the base of this mode of education. Its educative character came from the fact that these things were not learned for an immediate practical–professional purpose . . . One doesn't learn Latin and Greek in order to speak them, to become a waiter, or an interpreter, or whatever. One learns them in order to know the civilizations of Greece and Rome, whose existence is posited as a foundation of world culture. Latin or Greek is learned by way of grammar, somewhat mechanically; but the charges of mechanistic aridity are greatly exaggerated. This issue concerns children; they should be made to acquire certain habits of diligence, precision, physical composure, mental concentration on particular objects. Would a thirty- or forty-year-old scholar be able to sit at a desk for sixteen hours on end if, as a child, he had not acquired "compulsorily," through "mechanical coercion," the appropriate psycho-physical habits? This is where one has to start if one also wants to bring up scholars, and pressure must be applied across the board in order to produce those thousands, or hundreds, or even just dozens of first-rate scholars that every civilization requires . . .

Latin is learned, and it is analyzed down to its smallest basic units; it is analyzed as a dead thing. This is true, but every analysis carried out by a child is bound to be an analysis of a dead thing. Besides, one must not forget that, wherever Latin is studied in these ways, the life of the Romans is a myth that, to a certain extent, has already interested and still interests the child. The language is dead, it is dissected like a cadaver, it is true, but the cadaver comes back to life continually in the examples and the stories. Could one do the same with Italian? Impossible. No living language could be studied in the same way as Latin: it would be or *would seem* absurd. No child knows Latin when he starts to study it with this kind of analytic method. A living language could be known, and it would take just one child who knows it to break the spell: everybody would rush to the Berlitz school. Latin and Greek appear to the imagination like a myth, even for the teacher.[3]

Gramsci's discussion is one of many contributions to the long process of the revaluation of classical antiquity and its legacy. This was always a complicated issue; at least since the Renaissance, there has never been a time when classical knowledge has been wholly unproblematic, or when its value, and the nature of the benefits to be gained from acquiring such knowledge, could be taken for granted.[4] However, it is generally recognized that the value attached to the legacy of antiquity has come under particular scrutiny over the last century or so; at the very least, ideas about *why* knowledge of antiquity might be useful or relevant, and the degree to which these ideas are accepted within society at large, have changed radically. Gramsci notes the prevailing preference in the early twentieth century for an "instrumental" approach to education, one focused solely on the immediate interests (primarily material) of society, resulting in the abandonment or degrading of the study of the classics. Even in the nineteenth century, writers had begun to argue against the dominance of classics in the educational system, in favor of lessons that were more obviously and directly useful to the mass of the population.[5] In the twentieth century the study of antiquity came rapidly to be seen as a luxury, scarcely relevant to present concerns, and this perception had direct implications for the place of classics in school and university education and in the culture at large.[6]

This can be seen as the triumph of "modern" over "ancient" knowledge, the closing stages of a conflict that dated back to at least the seventeenth century with William Temple's "Essay Upon the Ancient and Modern Learning" and the subsequent scholarly debate. Modern mathematics, natural history, medicine, theology, history, and philosophy all claimed to have accumulated insights that went beyond – if not far beyond – those offered by classical writers; in subsequent centuries, disciplines like economics, offering ways of making sense of the world of which the ancients had never conceived, added to the clamor against the overvaluation of inherited knowledge and tradition. Increasingly, "modern" became a term of unequivocal approbation, denoting relevance and importance, rather than a neutral temporal description; in science, and increasingly in other disciplines, the most recent insights were usually valued more highly than those which they replaced. Modern knowledge was manifestly more useful and effective, as it transformed the present in visible, overwhelmingly impressive ways through the application of science and the rational organization of society and economy. It was natural, then, that modern knowledge should be preferred to the knowledge inherited from antiquity, and that the study of the society that had produced the works of the ancient authors should seem less relevant to the needs of modern society.

This is a familiar story for classicists, as are the arguments that can be marshaled against this attitude; Gramsci's rejection of an instrumental, anti-humanistic approach to education, and even his recommendation of the study of the classics as a means of developing the "transferable skills" and discipline required for diligent scholarly work, find plenty of analogies in defenses of classical learning in more recent educational debates. However, it is Gramsci's *defense* of the importance of studying the classical world that seems most telling. What is striking is his insistence on the absolute lack of any connection between antiquity and the present. The study of antiquity is useful, he argues, because antiquity is entirely dead. Its languages are a useful medium for education precisely because they are no longer living; the world of antiquity can be used as a subject of analysis and debate because it has no connection with the present. "One does not study Latin in order to learn Latin; it is studied in order to accustom children to studying, to analyzing a body of history that can be treated as a cadaver but returns continually to life"; however, this history, this reanimated society, does not have any relationship to the life of the present, but exists simply as a set of stories and examples, a collection of myths, that can capture the child's imagination. From this the child may learn the necessary skills to understand and criticize contemporary society, but there is nothing in the *content* of these stories that seems to have any bearing on the present, for all that they are "posited" as a foundation of world culture. In other words, Gramsci's defense of classical education shares the assumption of its detractors that knowledge of antiquity in and of itself is essentially irrelevant to understanding the present.

It was not simply that modern knowledge had gone beyond ancient; modern knowledge was relevant to the understanding of modern society in a way that classical learning could never be because modern society was radically different from that of any preceding period. Gramsci suggests that "in modern civilization all practical activities have become so complex and the sciences so intertwined with life that each activity tends to create a school for its own specialists."[7] This tendency to specialization is offered as an explanation for the decline of classics, but it could equally well serve as a justification for it; the nature of the modern world, and above all its complexity, is such that only modern knowledge is appropriate or adequate for its understanding. Classical learning speaks of and to a simpler world, which could be adequately comprehended as a whole by an individual without the need for the fragmentation of knowledge into diverse specialisms; antiquity itself was such a world, and so too were the medieval and Renaissance societies that had looked to the classics for answers. Under the conditions of the present, such worlds must seem either mythical or dead, absolutely separate from modernity.

From the nineteenth century onwards, the term "modern" became a marker no longer just of chronology, denoting a straightforward contrast with "ancient" or "medieval," but of quality, evaluated in almost invariably positive terms.[8] From this perspective, the science of the seventeenth century, the philosophy of the eighteenth, and the economy of the nineteenth could all be claimed as recognizably "modern" knowledge, in contrast to what had gone before. Further, there was a prevalent belief that all parts of "modern society" share in and reflect this quality of modernity; even if "modernity" is understood as primarily an economic phenomenon, for example, its effects are assumed to permeate the rest of society, culture, and individual behavior. The contrast between "modern" and "pre-modern" takes on greater significance than the more straightforward contrast between "present" and "past"; the more recent past could be seen as part of "our age," as modern or proto-modern, while earlier periods were regarded as entirely "other." The contrast had a spatial dimension as well; modernity was located primarily in Europe and the New World, while Africa and Asia were associated with the pre-modern past. Inevitably, then, there was a growing sense that pre-modern societies could have little direct relevance to the present. As Reinhart Koselleck expressed it in his study of the decline of the notion of *historia magistra vitae* (history, the teacher of life), in the course of the nineteenth century the gap between the "space of experience" and the "horizon of expectation" grew ever larger.[9] Belief in the exemplarity of the past, in its usefulness as a guide to future action, depended on the assumption that past and present occupied a continuous space of potential experience, founded on the supposed constancy of human nature, human behavior, and their social and physical context. This assumption was increasingly felt to be untenable. Koselleck emphasizes the importance for this development of the French Revolution, which was experienced as the start of a future that had never before existed – a new politics, a new society, a new type of individual – but one could equally well point to the more gradual impact of economic and technological change, which transformed not only social and economic structures, but nature itself. Such was the pace of change that even individual experience might be seen as an inadequate means of understanding the present or predicting the future; the wisdom of one generation could be rejected as irrelevant to the problems faced by the next. The accumulated experience of classical antiquity, addressing a simpler world that had wholly ceased to exist, could scarcely have anything to contribute to the desperate struggle to make sense of an unpredictable, infinitely complex modernity.

This perspective did not do away altogether with the idea that knowledge of the past in general and of classical antiquity in particular might still be relevant and important, but it changed the basis on which the classics might claim attention. Its domain shrank. It had next to nothing to contribute to the development of modern science and technology, and increasingly the "human sciences" like economics and sociology argued that evidence drawn from modern society itself was a more reliable basis for understanding, without any need to consider material from a society constituted on quite different principles. In history and philosophy, antiquity could maintain its place, and it continued to claim validity in the fields of art and culture – largely by detaching ancient cultural products from their original context and elevating them to the status of timeless classics, relevant to and open to appropriation by modernity. Even here, however, the position of antiquity was not unassailable. It was confronted not only by the complaints of modern artists against the normative status of the classics but also by the sense that much of ancient literature was scarcely worthy of "classic" status – as Goldhill suggests of Plutarch, it was incapable of performing its intended function in an alien setting, and could only be found boring by a modern reader without the scholarly expertise and inclination to consider it in its original context.[10] Both the emphasis – exemplified by Gramsci's discussion – on ancient literature and history as an inert body of material upon which a student can practice techniques of analysis that will later be turned to more practical uses in the "real" world, and the turn to studies of the reception of antiquity – insisting on its ongoing contribution to the development of modern culture – can be seen as the classicists' response to an ever-present threat of redundancy and irrelevance in the modern world.[11]

The Modernity of Antiquity

The later period of antiquity was in essence entirely modern.
E. Meyer *Kleine Scriften zur Geschichtstheorie und zur wirtschaftsliche und politischen Geschichte des Altertums*, 89

The belief that we are now living within modernity affected not only the status of the study of classical antiquity but also the ways in which classical antiquity itself was understood; it provoked new questions and debates about the nature of ancient society as well as how it should be analyzed. On the one hand, it became natural for many historians to see antiquity as "pre-modern," largely or entirely different and separate from the present. Such a society needed to be understood in its own terms, and historians therefore needed to map out the nature and significance of the ways that it differed from more recent and more familiar societies. They might look for new tools of analysis for this purpose – comparative evidence from other pre-modern or pre-industrial societies, for example – or at any rate, firmly reject the employment of theories, like economics, that had been created to understand the modern world. Above all, historians could now see in sharp relief the way that earlier generations had unconsciously created an antiquity in their own image, assuming it to be similar to their own society rather than realizing how far it was entirely "other." On the other hand, in so far as "modernity" could be seen as a quality rather than an exclusively temporal label, and because the differences between classical antiquity and other pre-modern societies seemed to be at least as significant as the differences between antiquity and the present, it was entirely possible for some historians to see classical civilization as being in some sense "modern," an earlier occurrence of the same phenomenon that was now being experienced in the present.

The obvious example of this dialectic is found in ancient economic history, an approach to understanding the past that was of course itself entirely modern, inconceivable before the mid-eighteenth century. Ancient historians were in fact slow to respond to the challenge and opportunities presented by the new science of political economy, despite the close relationship of writers like Edward Gibbon and George Grote to some of the pioneering economic thinkers.[12] When they did turn their attention to the economic and social aspects of Greek and Roman history, rather than focusing solely on the political and military, their arguments rapidly fell into the two positions that have dominated the subject ever since. Generally labeled as "primitivism" and "modernizing," these approaches focus entirely on the question of whether or not the ancient economy can be characterized as "modern," and whether the differences between ancient and modern should be seen as merely quantitative rather than qualitative.[13]

To a historian like M. I. Rostovtzeff, classical antiquity appeared, in important respects, to resemble the early modern period.[14] Clearly it could not match the scale of productive activity or international commerce of the present, but it was undoubtedly a world of widespread and sophisticated trade, thriving cities, innovations in agricultural production and the legal framework that supported economic transactions, a high level of monetization, and above all, a rich and complex material culture enjoyed not only by the wealthy elite but by the mass of the population. The cities of Hellenistic Greece and the Roman Empire were made glorious by the benefactions of a new class, whose wealth came from trade and manufacturing rather than traditional land-holding. All of this echoed the conditions that had nurtured the rise of capitalism in the late medieval and early modern periods, and foreshadowed subsequent developments.

The creation of a uniform world-wide civilization and of similar social and economic conditions is now going on before our eyes over the whole expanse of the civilized world. This process is complicated, and it is often difficult to clear up our minds about it. We ought therefore to keep in view that the ancient world also lived, for a series of centuries, a life which was uniform in culture and politics, in social and economic conditions. The modern development, in this sense, differs from the ancient only in quantity and not in quality.[15]

In contrast, a "primitivist" historian like M. I. Finley can seem to offer less a positive characterization of the ancient economy than a fervent reiteration of what it was *not* – namely, that it was not modern.[16] The scale of productive activity and trade is played down, with scepticism about the value of the archaeological evidence which Rostovtzeff valued so highly; it is emphasized that such activity was only a thin veneer on the surface of the agrarian subsistence economy in which the vast majority of the ancient population was engaged, and that the activity was inspired by quite different motivations from modern capitalism – the satisfaction of needs and the pursuit of status, not the relentless drive for unlimited profit. Ancient cities were dominated by the old land-owning elite and founded on consumption rather than production; there is no trace of any alternative set of values to the traditional disparagement of trade and industry as incompatible with honor and culture. Antiquity was not and could never have been the birthplace of modernity or capitalism, and it certainly was not modern. Further, this conclusion had important methodological implications; whereas Rostovtzeff was happy to use terms such as "bourgeoisie" to describe the urban elites of the Greek East, for Finley this, like any attempt at interpreting antiquity through the categories of modern economics, was an entirely illegitimate "modernizing" of the pre-modern past.

A number of different factors underlie and determine the parameters of this debate; one reason, perhaps, why it has proved to be so long-lived, despite the growing frustration of historians with its limitations. Partly, it reflects preferences for different sorts of evidence: the material record with its remnants of tens of thousands of amphorae and hundreds of shipwrecks versus the literary evidence that expressed the entirely non-modern world view of the ancient landowning elite. Partly, one might suggest, it reflects differences in temperament and in attitudes (emotional and political) towards modernity; Rostovtzeff's approach to antiquity is overwhelmingly optimistic in his evaluation of its level of development, in contrast to his pessimistic view of the likely fate of European civilization, whereas Finley takes a minimalist and almost cynical view of the potential significance of every piece of evidence, and is constantly struck by differences where Rostovtzeff sees similarities and analogies. Their accounts rest also on different interpretations of the dynamic of human history on the global scale; whereas Rostovtzeff believes in the possibility of recurrence, a perspective that resembles the view of history as the birth, maturity, and decadence of successive civilizations popularized by writers like Oswald Spengler, Finley's narrative is a linear one focused around a single abrupt change in continuity between the stagnant pre-modern and the dynamic modern.

Above all, however, these two versions rest on quite different conceptions of the nature of modernity. Rostovtzeff's approach might be labelled "phenomenological"; modernity is understood in terms of a set of distinctive features, such as trade, flourishing cities, productive activity, and so forth. The past can be labeled as "modern" when it exhibits similar features, and in these terms classical antiquity, above all the Roman Empire, seems to have a strong claim to the title. The alternative approach, that taken by Finley, is to insist that modernity should be understood as a coherent, interconnected system; its characteristic features of trade, flourishing cities, and so forth are not accidental but closely connected to and dependent on one another, determined by a single underlying principle. Modernity is not, as it seems to be for Rostovtzeff, a collection of powerful but disconnected images and conceptions of "the modern," but a unified, unique development. The surface resemblance between antiquity and the early modern period is irrelevant if their underlying principles of organization were different, as Finley argues that they were. The same logic applies to the use of "modern" terminology in characterizing the ancient world; whereas Rostovtzeff wants to use "bourgeoisie" as a general term of social analysis applicable to any social system, Finley and the primitivists insist that its range of reference is limited to early modern proto-capitalist and modern capitalist society. Use of the term in an ancient context implies not that some characteristics of both the ancient and the modern social group are comparable, but that all of them are, and that in turn implies that antiquity was a modern capitalist society.

The intention of this discussion is not so much to suggest that the modernizing position is less wrong than the "primitivists" have maintained, as to argue that it is problematic for different reasons than they suggest, and that the primitivist position is equally misleading for very similar reasons. The archaeologist Andrea Carandini argued twenty years ago that " 'modernism' and 'primitivism' are two sides to the same coin, the self-deification of the present and the annihilation of the past."[17] That seems to imply that the comparison between past and present, whether implicit or explicit, positive or negative, may be the problem; scarcely a tenable position when most theories of historical knowledge would insist on the impossibility of understanding the past except through knowledge and experience of the present. The problem is rather that of the idea of "modernity" itself. The modernizers and primitivists tend to talk past one another because they have entirely different ideas of what modernity is and how it could be identified; however, neither side recognizes this as an issue, either in their own work or in that of their opponents. Each takes "modernity" as something that is straightforward and known, an empirical object with which antiquity can be compared and contrasted and against which its performance can be measured. This assumption is by no means confined to ancient economic history, though it is more visible there; it pervades all discussions of antiquity, including the new discipline of "reception studies." Accounts of the changing meanings and interpretations of classical texts in the nineteenth and twentieth centuries all too often consider them in the "context" of a simplistic and under-analyzed notion of modernity, whose existence and nature is taken for granted. A clear example is found in Goldhill's assertion, in an otherwise highly sophisticated and self-aware analysis of the changing meanings and significance of knowledge of Greek since the Renaissance, that "a modern reader" must find Plutarch boring.[18] It is true enough that Plutarch's popularity has declined rapidly, especially since 1850, but attributing this simply to "modernity" seems insufficient, given the lack of any agreement as to what "modernity" might be.

The Problem of Modernity

The problems created by the existence of different approaches to under-standing modernity are not confined to ancient history. Throughout the human sciences there is no consensus, no single agreed definition or theory, and yet it is taken for granted not only that modernity exists but that it has been the defining condition of existence since, at the very least, the beginning of the nineteenth century. Understanding of what it means to be modern (and hence by implication not-modern) has varied from discipline to discipline, from century to century, and from country to country. Rather than different theories addressing the same object, in the case of "modernity" the different theories work to create the object of their analysis, and are thus largely or wholly incomparable with one another.

The tensions evident in the debate on the "modernity" of the ancient economy are replicated in attempts at getting to grips with modernity itself. Is it to be seen as a unique, temporally located phenomenon, a particular stage in a linear process of historical development, or a quality that is most easily identified in the present but could be found elsewhere? The sociologist Anthony Giddens opens his study of the theme from the former perspective:

> "Modernity" refers to modes of social life or organization which emerged in Europe from about the seventeenth century onwards and which subsequently became more or less worldwide in their influence. This associates modernity with a time period and with an initial geographical location, but for the moment leaves its major characteristics safely stowed away in a black box.[19]

However, this approach involves all the usual risks of periodization: it rests on the assumption, common to many accounts of modernity, that the temporal juxtaposition of different social structures, institutions, and practices automatically implies their coherence and interconnection, while the question of how to define the chronological limits of the phenomenon rests on an already-existing idea of what is to be bounded.[20] Essentially, Giddens' argument seeks to start from the fact that there is general agreement both that we live within modernity and about its major elements, and then aims to develop a more nuanced account of the phenomenon. This begs questions not only about the Eurocentric implications of the account, as Goody has argued, since the individual elements that are often considered distinctively modern can be paralleled in other societies, but also about the status of "modernity" as a taken-for-granted object of analysis.[21]

The "phenomenological" approach to modernity, identifying it in terms of the characteristics which are generally associated with "modern" society, is common enough; Agnes Heller defines it in terms of two "constituents" and three "logics," while Giddens identifies four "frameworks of experience."[22]

Each of these approaches is fascinating and persuasive in its own terms, but it is striking how varied the lists of the "characteristic" features of modernity can be. The pervasive sense that we are living in modernity means that virtually any aspect of contemporary existence can be regarded as symptomatic of this, and further assumed to be somehow connected with every other aspect. Different disciplines make their own selections from the list of potentially defining characteristics; "modernity" defined in economic terms, therefore, overlaps only slightly with the modernity studied by social theory, and different interpretative traditions within those disciplines are equally inclined to privilege different aspects of "modern life" in constituting their object of analysis.

It is scarcely surprising, therefore, that the attempts at discerning the underlying logic of modernity, the force or forces that are assumed to explain and unify what is otherwise experienced as complex, chaotic, and incoherent, have reached such different conclusions. Such theories argue simultaneously for the validity of their methods and assumptions on the grounds of their success in producing an interpretation of modernity that chimes with lived experience and for the validity of their interpretations of the present on the basis of the claims to authority of their chosen approach. Is modernity to be located in the structures of economic production and their role in determining the material conditions of life, or in the lived experience of social individuals – themes such as alienation, fragmentation, depersonalization, *anomie* – or in a characteristic psychology? The result of such debates is often an image or a metaphor, powerful and persuasive but unfalsifiable and incomparable with other such images, as Giddens compares the "iron cage" of Max Weber and the "devouring monster" of Karl Marx and then proposes his own interpretation of modernity as juggernaut, "a runaway engine of enormous power which, collectively as human beings, we can drive to some extent but which also threatens to rush out of control and which can rend itself asunder."[23]

For social science, of course, the development of these multiple interpretations of modernity can be taken as an interesting question in itself. The real problems arise whenever social scientists, or anyone else, seek to draw on the concept of modernity as a basis for interpretation and explanation, a means of understanding a particular aspect of "modern society" – if only in order to explain the way that an ancient text was read in a new context. Since modernity is understood, and indeed experienced, as a unified phenomenon, theories of its nature and underlying laws of motion make powerful claims about their potential to explain all aspects of modern life. If modernity is ultimately defined and constituted by, say, the progressive rationalization of society or the class struggle between bourgeoisie and proletariat, then this insight can illuminate everything from drug-taking and urban violence to the development of the English novel. But that is a large "if"; there are always plenty of other interpretations of modernity available, "as many versions as there are thinkers or journalists."[24] The question must always be: Which modernity? Whose theory of it?

"Modernity" is protean; it changes shape according to whether it is viewed as a historical phenomenon or as a quality, and according to whether it is seen from an economic, a social or a psychological perspective, through the theories of Marx, Nietzsche, Weber, Freud, or many others. Our lives, experiences, and even emotions are felt to be determined by the fact that we live in modern times; but it is equally possible to argue, with Bruno Latour, that we have never actually been modern.[25] Modernity can be seen as a mythology, a set of stories that are called upon to give legitimacy to institutions or actions and to give meaning to our lives and experiences. As Nietzsche argued, the fact that a mythology is not actually true, and that it can be shown to be entirely self-serving and simply a reflection of our own desires, does not thereby lessen its importance or effectiveness.[26] The defining, unifying feature of modernity, one might argue, is the conviction of its own existence and significance; the sense, of those who believe themselves to be modern and to live in modern times, that this explains the whole of their condition of existence, including their dissatisfaction with the world and with themselves. If modernity is "only" an idea, it has proved an astonishingly powerful and influential one.

Future, Present, Past

It is possible to identify a unifying theme within the many various theories of modernity, besides their conviction that they are engaged with a real, knowable object: a particular relation to time and history. This is often suggested as one of the defining characteristics of the experience of modernity itself: it is characterized by unceasing change and transformation – "all that is solid evaporates," as Marx put it – in contrast to the unchanging past, or by the regulation of time through the widespread use of the clock, a view which can be dated at least as far back as Oswald Spengler's denunciation of the Germans for inventing this "spine-chilling symbol of time ticking away."[27] The archetypal modern attitude is a sense of separation from the past, based on the unique qualities of "newness" possessed by the present; the abandonment of the historical perspective in the social sciences can be seen as the working through of Hegel's forthright statement:

> One refers rulers, statesmen and peoples to the lessons of the experience of history. However, what experience and history teach is this, that peoples and governments have never learnt anything from history, nor have they ever acted in accordance with the lessons which could be drawn from it. Each period has such peculiar circumstances and is such an individual situation that decisions must be made and can only be made on the basis of the period itself. In the crowd of world events a general principle is no help, nor is the recollection of similar conditions, because something like a pale memory has no strength against the liveliness and freedom of the present. From this perspective nothing is more insipid than the often-repeated appeal to Greek and Roman examples, as happened so frequently in the revolutionary period in France.[28]

Not only does the horizon of expectation, in Koselleck's terms, move ever further away from the space of experience, but distinctions are drawn even within the latter; the bulk of past events seems ever more separate from and irrelevant to our own experiences and expectations, but we may retain some connection with those societies that are past but still recognized as "modern." Ancient examples, however, have nothing to contribute to understanding the present, since that world was so radically different; whereas once men looked anxiously to the past for guidance, now modernity is moving towards its own self-understanding as the basis for complete self-reliance.

> Are we not entitled to assume that the achievements of modern times, our illumination and the progress of all arts and sciences, have worn out the Greek and Roman garments of their childhood and outgrown their leading-strings, so that they can now advance on their own territory without hindrance?[29]

> The philosopher, as he glances now to the past, now to the future, will perceive more and more striking differences between the social condition of our ancestors and that of our descendents . . . Hitherto men have walked backwards on the path of civilization, turning their backs on the future; they have usually had their gaze fixed on the past and they have glanced only very seldom and cursorily at the future.[30]

However bold such statements appear, and however detrimental to the status of the historical disciplines, this attitude did not in fact amount to a complete abandonment of the past. On the contrary, it established a new, and if anything more intimate, relationship with it, to the extent that modernity can be said to have no identity which does not depend on a relation to the past, understood now not as a source of examples and precepts but as the "other," which allowed modernity to define its own contours.

> If in one's own history it was possible to register new experiences, those which supposedly no one had ever before had, it was also possible to conceive the past as something that was fundamentally "other." This in turn led to the fact that it was precisely along the plane of progress that the specificity of the epoch had to be expressed. Hence, diagnosis of the *neue Zeit* and analysis of the past eras corresponded to each other.[31]

In the first place, the past was required as a means of measuring change, of establishing the degree to which modernity was indeed an entirely new form of society. The sense that modernity is characterized by an unprecedented degree of upheaval and constant transformation rests on an implicit image of past timelessness and stability; modernity is defined both by its own internal changeability and by the change from an unchanging past. Giddens' comment, for example, that "we get only limited assistance from our knowledge of prior periods of transition" because of the unprecedented degree of transformation in modernity, is slightly undercut by the temporal references inherent in statements like "in both their extensionality and their intensionality the transformations involved in modernity are more profound than most sorts of change characteristic of prior periods."[32] The past continues to be required as a point of reference, to calculate the speed of change and the distance covered from the point of origin – the more distant the past appears, the greater modernity's success.

Second, the past thereby becomes a means of understanding change, precisely through understanding the nature of the differences between past and present. Exemplarity is abandoned; the past matters because it is different and thus represents a means of discerning the essential characteristics of modernity and the process of its development. This was explicitly recognized by many of the pioneering theorists of modernity, who did not share the view that the past had nothing to teach the present about itself.

The observation of the present state of civilization, considered by itself, can no more determine the actual tendencies of society, than the study of any other isolated epoch can do . . . The chronological order of historical epochs is not their philosophical order. In place of saying; the past, the present and the future, we should say the past, the future and the present. In truth it is only when we have conceived the future by the aid of the past that we can with advantage revert to the present so as to seize its true character.[33]

The observer's eye may acquire a singular acuteness by the comparative study of as many nations as possible, especially of those which have already passed away. [If anyone could] contemplate the history of mankind as a whole, of which the histories of individual nations are but the parts, the successive steps in the evolution of humanity, would of course afford him a similar objective rule for all those points in which whole peoples permanently differ from one another.[34]

Finally, the past offered a means of developing a critique of modernity, by providing a measure against which change might be not only measured but evaluated. It represented, potentially, an alternative to the present – if not one that could ever realistically be revived, then at any rate a basis for imagining future possibilities. The problem for most critics of modernity, as Habermas notes of Hegel's interpretation, is that the present seen as the outcome of natural processes of change cannot be criticized or evaluated on any terms other than its own, and so offers no grounds for imagining alternatives to it.[35] Comparison and contrast with the past, however, might offer a basis for questioning whether the process was indeed natural and inevitable, or whether, on the contrary, it was a perversion of the true destiny of humanity. The contrast may reveal what has been lost as well as gained in the process, and so allow modernity to be held to account for its failure to live up to its promises. Above all, the past shows that things were once different; logically, then, the present state of affairs cannot be assumed to be an eternal condition, and there are grounds for hope, for those dissatisfied with the consequences of modernity, that the future might be different in turn.

In the classical period of the theorizing of modernity, the past most often called upon for these purposes was the world of Greece and Rome, especially the former. In part this undoubtedly reflects the contingent fact that classics dominated the education of most thinkers in the nineteenth century and, in Germany at least, well into the twentieth.[36] It was entirely natural for them to have recourse to classical examples and to think of issues to some extent in the terms in which they were discussed by the ancient authors, with whom they were so familiar. More recent writers on the subject are likely to operate with a less specific idea of "pre-modern societies" or "agrarian civilizations" as the basis for the contrast with modernity; even so, references to classical authors, especially philosophers, persist to a significant degree, and the classical world continues to provide images and concepts, like the term "agora," as a means of characterizing a particular relationship between the public and private spheres.[37] Classical antiquity might make for a particularly good example not only because of its familiarity – in the eighteenth and nineteenth centuries it was by far the best known pre-modern society – but because of its nature. It was, one might suggest, conceived to be sufficiently similar to the present for the comparison to yield precise and nuanced knowledge; unlike the crude contrast between, say, modern Europe and nineteenth-century Africa, comparison of the sophisticated yet clearly different society and economy of classical antiquity with that of modernity would throw the particular characteristics of the latter into sharp relief. At any rate this seems to have been the prevalent assumption, fuelled by the racism that regarded the ancient Mediterranean as the place of origin of European civilization and other cultures as wholly, rather than partially, primitive and "other."

Eighteenth- and nineteenth-century discussions of the nature of modernity, whether understood in economic, social, or cultural terms, constantly refer to classical examples, texts, and ideas; the modern idea of modernity is inconceivable without the background of antiquity. The obvious problem with such approaches, of course, is that they almost invariably assume the existence of a knowable and largely known antiquity that can serve as a counterpoint to a nebulous, still-to-be-defined modernity, and bring its outline into clarity. This was quite as much an illusion as the belief of classicists and ancient historians in a stable, clearly defined modernity, against which they could measure and evaluate the ancient world. Ideas of "antiquity" shifted and were constantly renegotiated, in response to new evidence, new preferences, and new knowledge – as the new sciences of modernity in turn influenced the way that antiquity was interpreted. The concepts of "antiquity" and "modernity" are equally implicated in one another, equally ambiguous and mobile.

Untimely Knowledge

For Nietzsche, knowledge about antiquity is important because it is "untimely," able to illuminate the present through comparison and contrast. It is worth noting that he was one of the few writers also to reverse the process; to recognize that "antiquity" was as unstable a concept as "modernity," with each informing and influencing the other, and to see this interdependence as both an opportunity and a threat. In the confrontation with modernity, the right idea of antiquity could be liberating; the wrong one might be fatal.

This book aims to consider the way that, in the "long nineteenth century," ideas of modernity were developed and explored through the consideration of the use of the classical past and the definition of differences, contrasts, and continuities. It does not attempt to offer a complete account of the idea of modernity, a truly gigantic task, or even a complete account of the role of antiquity in the development of that idea, but rather seeks to highlight relevant themes in a selection of the most important writers on the subject. Such a project invariably involves a number of risks; that of neglecting writers and texts whom others might think deserve a far more prominent place in the account; that of misinterpreting their ideas through too-brief treatment and by shoe-horning their views into debates in which they never intended to participate; and that of exaggerating the importance of the past, and the classical past in particular, in the development of these intellectual traditions. I have wondered on several occasions whether the importance of antiquity for the concept of modernity has genuinely been missed, or whether I tend to perceive it because of my own background and intellectual inclinations. I take heart from the fact that it is identified, and discussed from a different perspective, in at least some of the works which have inspired this book.

> Historical epochs, such as modernity or classical antiquity, are constructs that we design in order to highlight, through historical comparison, distinctive elements of any set of practices or institutions. With the "fetishism of modernities" these conceptual constraints come back to haunt us as the real-world obstacles to our goals.[38]

The next three chapters consider three different, though frequently interconnected, ways in which the example of antiquity was felt to illuminate the special qualities of modernity, whether positively or negatively: in the organization of production and economic life; in the nature of social relationships and organization and of the human individual; and in the development of culture and its functions within society. The fifth chapter will consider the development of attitudes to history as a whole, both the attempts at discerning the overall logic of its development and the suspicion that the historical sense itself might represent a distinctively modern problem or a problem for modernity. The final chapter will look at some of the issues involved in the deployment of antiquity in discussions of modernity, not just as the basis for substantive social analysis but as a rhetorical strategy, focusing on the key example of the way that ancient slavery was discussed and represented.

Can the past illuminate the present or predict the future? Since our understanding of the past derives from our knowledge and experience of the present, to the extent that, in Nietzsche's view, it is no more than the projection and externalization of our own desires, this seems doubtful; and yet, insofar as any sense has been made of "modernity," it has been through the confrontation and mutual interrogation of those two mythological constructs, antiquity and modernity. Nietzsche's critique of contemporary philology and its distortion of both past and present, like Marx's analysis of the way that the past could be employed to defend the present and destroy the future, did not lead either of them to abandon consideration of classical antiquity. What mattered, and matters, is how and why antiquity is considered. "For I do not know what meaning classical studies would have in our time if not that of working in their untimeliness – that is to say, against our time and thereby on our time and, let us hope, for the benefit of a time to come."[39]

Notes

1   Davidson (1977); Entwhistle (1979).
2   *Prison Notebooks*, IV, §49.
3   *Ibid.*, §55.
4   Goldhill (2002).
5   Cf. Rosen (1989).
6   Marchand (1996), 341–75; Stray (1998).
7   *Prison Notebooks*, IV, §49.
8   Williams (1983), 208–9.

9 Koselleck (2004), 26–42, 255–75.
10 Goldhill (2002), 292.
11 Cf. Martindale (2006).
12 Morley (1998).
13 Morley (2004a), 33–50.
14 On Rostovtzeff, see Shaw (1992).
15 Rostovtzeff (1926), 10.
16 See above all Finley (1985).
17 Carandini (1983), 202.
18 Goldhill (2002), 292.
19 Giddens (1990), 1.
20 Cf. Goody (2004), 6–15.
21 Goody (2004), 6.
22 Heller (1999); Giddens (1990), 137–44. Cf. also Hall, Held, Hubert, and Thompson (1995).
23 Giddens (1990), 144.
24 Latour (1993), 10.
25 Latour (1993).
26 *Vom Nutzen und Nachtheil der Historie für das Leben.*
27 *Der Untergand des Abendlandes,* 19, and cf. 10–11 on differences between modern and ancient experiences of time. Giddens (1990), 17–21; Harvey (1989), 10–38.
28 Hegel, *Vorlesungen über die Philosophie der Geschichte,* 17.
29 Hegel, "On classical studies," 324.
30 Saint-Simon, "Social organisation," 221–2.
31 Koselleck (2004), 240.
32 Giddens (1990), 4–5.
33 Comte, "Plan of the scientific operations," 151–2.
34 Roscher, *Principles of Political Economy,* 114–15.
35 Habermas (1987), 16–22.
36 See e.g. McCarthy (1994), (2003).
37 Bauman (2000), 39.
38 Yack (1992), xiv.
39 Nietzsche, *Vom Nutzen und Nachtheil der Historie für das Leben,* 247.

2

The Great Transformation
Ancient and Modern Economics

[The bourgeoisie] has been the first to show what man's activity can bring
about. It has accomplished marvels wholly different from Egyptian pyramids,
Roman aqueducts and Gothic cathedrals.
K. Marx and F. Engels, *Manifest der Kommunistischen Partei*, 465

The *Manifesto of the Communist Party* of 1848, credited to both Karl Marx
and Friedrich Engels but largely written by the former, offers not only a
searching critique of the nature of the modern world and a call for the
overthrow of its creators, the *bourgeoisie*, but also, perhaps more surprisingly, a passionate and evocative celebration of its achievement.[1] The
Manifesto presents – with, as Marshall Berman has pointed out, far greater
eloquence than any of those committed to the status quo had ever
managed – a vision of the overwhelming material power of modernity, dwarfing even the greatest achievements of earlier ages, and its
liberation of human creativity from the constraints of nature. Underlying
this transformation of the world, in Marx's account, is an economic transformation, unleashing the forces of modern production whose capacity
now vastly exceeds the provision of mere subsistence and basic goods
and whose reach extends far beyond the locality, the region, and even
the nation:

In place of the old needs, satisfied by local production, new ones appear,
which require for their satisfaction the products of the most distant lands
and climates. In place of the old local and national self-sufficiency and self-
containment appears a universal traffic, a universal dependence of nations
on one another.[2]

However, this transformation is not just a matter of the scale of modern economic activity in comparison with earlier periods, but of its nature. For Marx, societies need to be understood in terms of the way that they organize production; in the modern world this is qualitatively different from anything that has gone before, and that has far-reaching implications for the rest of society.

> The bourgeoisie cannot exist without continually revolutionising the instruments of production, and thereby the relations of production, and thereby the entirety of social relationships. Preservation of the old modes of production in unchanged form was in contrast the first condition of existence for all earlier industrial classes. The ongoing revolutionising of production, the constant unsettling of all social conditions, the eternal insecurity and movement uncertainty and agitation mark out the epoch of the bourgeoisie from all earlier ones. All firm, rusted-shut relations with their entourage of time-honoured ideas and opinions are dissolved, all new-formed ones become antiquated before they can ossify. Everything solid and permanent evaporates, everything holy is desecrated, and men's eyes are finally opened to the conditions in which they live and their relations with one another.[3]

Modernity, in Marx's account, is based on constant revolution and innovation, driven by the relentless competition inherent in capitalism, the modern mode of production, in which those who fail to change will quickly succumb to their rivals. Everything that might stand in the way of expanding production further will be swept away, not only in the economic sphere but in the wider society and culture. Whereas in earlier societies, such as classical Greece, economic activity had been firmly subjected to political and ethical constraints, in capitalism everything is subordinated to the drive for ever-increased profit. The result – at the expense of the human development of the individuals who are reduced to mere appendages of the productive machine – is the vast and apparently limitless expansion of the material power of humanity as a whole.

> The bourgeoisie has, in scarcely a hundred years of class-domination, created more massive and more colossal forces of production than all the preceding generations together. Subjugation of the forces of nature, machinery, application of chemistry to industry and agriculture, steam-navigation, railways, electric telegraphs, cultivation of entire continents, canalisation of rivers, whole populations conjured out of the ground – what earlier century had any idea that such forces of production slumbered in the lap of social labour?[4]

The Invention of the Modern Economy

Comparison with the past clearly lies at heart of this account of modernity, and of many others which understand the contemporary world in terms of its economic and material development.[5] The present is characterized above all by its material power, its ability to do unprecedented things on an unprecedented scale, something which is thrown into sharp relief through contrast with the limited capacity of earlier forms of society; the capacity of the modern world is then explained on the basis of the particular characteristics of its economic organization and of the "pre-modern" nature of earlier forms of production. The identification of the modern economy as the determining factor in the emergence of new conditions of existence rests equally on the reification of "the economy" as a distinct and significant area of human activity in all periods (even though the concept is an entirely modern one) and on the insistence that its modern manifestation was significantly different in both structure and effects from all that had gone before. Economic accounts of modernity, to a far greater extent than social or political ones, often identify a dramatic discontinuity in historical development separating the modern from earlier periods; a "great transformation," located initially and primarily in the economic sphere but affecting all aspects of human life.[6] Two of the most important interpretations of the nature and development of modernity, those of Karl Marx and Max Weber, place this economic transformation at the heart, or close to the heart, of their arguments.

In retrospect, it seems that modernity took a long time to recognize its economic superiority over earlier societies; contemporary commentators remained largely oblivious to the "great transformation" until well after the period when most historians would now consider its effects to have become unmistakable. Eighteenth-century arguments about the effects of increasing "luxury" on the nation – debates which can now be seen as, in part, a confused response to the visible consequences of the economic transformation in patterns of trade, consumption, and national prosperity – took it for granted that contemporary society was, at least in material terms, fully comparable to its predecessors, and that discussion of contemporary issues would invariably require the consideration of parallels with the past, above all classical antiquity.[7] Contributors to this debate constantly invoked classical precedents, both in their frequent citations from ancient denunciations of luxury, like those of Cicero and

Seneca, and in the pseudonyms that they adopted for their publications, such as Civis and Britannicus. For many of them, the increased availability of material goods for the mass of the population and the degree of "refinement" now enjoyed by the wealthier sections of British society represented not an unprecedented development, to be explained by changes in the organization of production or trade, but a straightforward return to the conditions of imperial Rome.[8] Antiquity was the great exemplar of the disastrous consequences of luxuriousness for military prowess, sexual continence, and political liberty, and hence the obvious model for understanding contemporary developments and their likely terminus.[9] On the other hand, antiquity was also the yardstick for frugality, virtue, and the philosophical denunciation of luxury; other commentators argued with equal seriousness that the classical world was manifestly superior, in the size of its population and its material power as well as in its moral and cultural life, compared with the degeneracy of the present.[10] What was not in dispute was that antiquity was the obvious, if not inevitable, point of reference and comparison for the debate.

Those who rejected this pessimistic account of the state of contemporary society and the social impact of increasing prosperity employed a variety of arguments in addressing the classical material. This included the revaluation of the standard exemplars of classical frugality ("Of what benefit was Sparta to Greece? Did she ever have a Demosthenes, Sophocles, Apelles, or Phidias?");[11] the reinterpretation of ancient history ("It would be easy to prove, that these writers mistook the cause of the disorders in the Roman state, and ascrib'd to luxury and the arts what really proceeded from an ill model'd government, and the unlimited extent of conquests");[12] and, in the case of the Scottish philosopher David Hume's famous essay "On the populousness of antient nations," the critical examination of evidence for ancient population size to undermine the assertions of his opponents both that periods of antiquity were better populated than the present day and that this was due to their freedom from luxury. More positively, writers of the Scottish Enlightenment sought to refocus the debate, and above all to sideline its moralizing dimension, by redefining and historicizing the ideas of luxury and necessity:

> A linen shirt, for example, is strictly speaking not a necessary of life. The Greeks and Romans lived, I suppose, very comfortably though they had no linen. But in the present times, through the greater part of Europe, a creditable day-labourer would be ashamed to appear in public without a

linen shirt, the want of which would be supposed to denote that disgraceful degree of poverty, which, it is presumed, no one can well fall into without extreme bad conduct.[13]

Hand in hand with the historicization of "luxury" came a new insistence on the existence of significant differences between past and present in material terms, to the advantage of the present, which thereby undermined arguments based on direct comparisons between ancient and modern luxuriousness. Hume offered this as a clear reason why one might be skeptical about the claim that antiquity must have been more populous:

> There are many other circumstances in which ancient nations seem inferior to the modern, both for the happiness and encrease of mankind. Trade, manufactures, industry, were nowhere, in former ages, so flourishing as they are at present in Europe. The only garb of the ancients, both for males and females, seems to have been a kind of flannel.[14]

> All our later improvements and refinements, have they done nothing towards the easy subsistence of men, and consequently towards their propagation and encrease? Our superior skill in mechanics; the discovery of new worlds by which commerce has been so much enlarged; the establishment of posts; and the use of bills of exchange: these seem all extremely useful to the encouragement of art, industry and populousness.[15]

Adam Smith's contribution to the debate had sought to focus attention on the social effects of "refinement," insisting on the need to consider the impact of any increase in commerce and consumption within its specific social and economic context. This then offered grounds for distinguishing between different sorts of "luxury," some of which could be evaluated positively, and for insisting that the same phenomenon might have different effects in different historical situations; it even offered the possibility of preserving the traditional account of ancient luxuriousness and its injurious consequences without implying that the contemporary world faced a similar fate. James Steuart, for example, argued that the wealth of Babylon, Persia, Greece, and Rome was the product of conquest and hence proved the ruin of those states, whereas the prosperity of cities like Carthage, Athens, and Alexandria was, like that of the present day, the product of industry and hence was a source of national strength.[16] Even in the case of Rome, Steuart argued, it was not luxury itself that brought about its downfall, but the organization of society:

Had the Roman Empire been governed with order and tranquillity, this taste of luxury, by precipitating money into the hands of the numerous classes, would, in time, have wrought the effects of multiplying the number of the industrious; consequently, of increasing the demand for vendible substance; consequently, of raising the price of it . . . But while either despotism or slavery were the patrimonial inheritance of every one on coming into the world, we are not to expect to see the same principles operate, as in ages where the monarch and the peasant are born equally free to enjoy the provision made for them by their forefathers.[17]

In developing their characterization of the differences between their own society and the present day, these early political economists focused on three factors: the policies of the state, the development of liberty, and the organization of production. The development of the modern economy, as seen in the increased variety of material goods of all kinds, was, they argued, not due to any attempt at regulation on the part of governments but to freedom from the restrictions that had previously shackled economic agents, whether these were official – "In antient times it was usual to attempt to regulate the profits of merchants and other dealers" – or a matter of cultural attitudes such as the depiction of trade and manufacturing as "slavish": "The policy of the ancient republics of Greece, and that of Rome, though it honoured agriculture more than manufactures or foreign trade, yet seems to have rather discouraged the latter employments than to have given any direct or intentional encouragement to the former."[18] These unproductive policies, and the attitudes of society in general towards productive activity, were closely linked to the institution of slavery, which was seen to have dominated the entire economy of the ancients, and which offered important lessons for the present:

To clarify the political ideas of the industrialists, to discover what industry must do today to improve its standing in society, it is necessary to enquire what point industry has reached at this moment in its political career. Now this can only be done by looking back at the past, by a brief recapitulation of the successive steps which industry has taken until now. If we go back in the history of industry to the Greeks and Romans, we find among these nations that the industrial class was completely enslaved by the military class.[19]

Ancient dependence on slavery had, it was argued, a number of consequences for ancient society and economy. It prevented the poor from finding employment; this kept them poor and meant that the market for manufactured goods was limited to the demands of the wealthy property owners, in contrast to the mass demand that was found in the modern economy. Further, while slavery might appear to be efficient and cost effective, this was an illusion:

> If great improvements are seldom to be expected from great proprietors, they are least of all to be expected when they employ slaves for their workmen. The experience of all ages and nations, I believe, demonstrates that the work done by slaves, though it appears to cost only their maintenance, is in the end the dearest of all. A person who can acquire no property can have no other interest but to eat as much and to labour as little as possible.[20]

The most that could be said for ancient slave labor, and hence for the ancient economy, was that it appeared in many cases to be less harsh and more flexible than contemporary American slavery, and indeed "as a temporary fact, in an early and rude state of the arts of life, it may have been a great accelerator of progress."[21] The fact that the practice of slavery continued in some areas of the modern world showed, of course, that economic progress was not complete or absolute; the ancient evidence was needed as much to show the direction in which the present ought to be developing, and the necessity of the abandonment of slavery, as to establish the basis of its difference from the past.

Consideration of slavery linked to the third factor which, according to the political economists, contributed to the superiority of the modern economy, namely significant improvements in the organization of production. This argument was founded on the crucial insight of Adam Smith into the impact of the division and specialization of labor and the possibilities this created for improving both the quality of the product and the efficiency of the production process. In the words of the opening chapter of *The Wealth of Nations*, "the greatest improvement in the productive powers of labour, and the greater part of the skill, dexterity, and judgment with which it is any where directed, or applied, seem to have been the effects of the division of labour."[22] This was seen to be the underlying basis for the extraordinary complexity of the structures that supported everyday life in a modern economy:

> Observe the accommodation of the most common artificer or day-labourer in a civilised and thriving country, and you will perceive that the number

of people of whose industry a part, though but a small part, has been
employed in procuring him this accommodation, exceeds all computation
. . . Without the assistance and co-operation of many thousands, the very
meanest person in a civilised country could not be provided, even according to, what we very falsely imagine, the easy and simple manner in which
he is accommodated.[23]

However, it is significant that Smith saw this development not as a sudden
transformation of the economy but as the emerging result of a long and
gradual process of change:

This division of labour, from which so many advantages are derived, is not
originally the effect of any human wisdom, which foresees and intends that
general opulence to which it gives occasion. It is the necessary, though very
slow and gradual consequence of a certain propensity in human nature which
has in view no such extensive utility; the propensity to truck, barter and
exchange one thing for another.[24]

It has been noted by many commentators that the classical political
economists failed to recognize the extent or the full significance of the
economic transformation that was taking place around them, and that in
particular they underestimated the impact of technological innovation.[25]
Far from perceiving the potential of new sources of power and labor-
saving devices to produce apparently unlimited growth in production
and productivity, Smith and his contemporaries assumed that sooner or
later even the dynamic British economy would return to a steady state of
equilibrium, just as had happened in every previous example of a society
experiencing economic expansion. For all that they insisted on the existence of significant differences between past and present economies, and
identified the factors that had brought about these developments, they
had no perception of an absolute distinction or discontinuity between
the modern world and its precursors. On the contrary, their accounts
were permeated with historical material, used for a variety of purposes –
to identify and illustrate general economic principles, to emphasize the
variety and variability of human behavior, and to criticize contemporary
policies on the basis of precedent and experience – and generally assuming an underlying continuity and comparability between past and present.
As Steuart argued, "let those who are versed in history lay circumstances
together and examine whether facts do not prove the truth of what I have
been saying."[26] Adam Smith, one of the first writers to suggest that the

natural order of the economy had "in all the modern states of Europe, been, in many respects, entirely inverted,"[27] was happy to draw on a miscellany of evidence from "antient times" in his analysis of the workings of the economy, a category which encompassed fifteenth-century Scotland, medieval England, and Britain at the time of Caesar's invasion.[28] Clear distinctions were drawn between different stages of economic development in human history, but these were characterized in terms of a progression from pastoralism to agriculture and then to commerce – a scheme which established classical antiquity, or certain parts of it, as comparable in its overall level of economic development to the present.[29] Modernity, at this stage in the debate, was not identified as a distinct or unprecedented phenomenon in economic terms.

The classical past, universally recognized as a high point of human material, social, and cultural development, was especially important for any economic argument which engaged with historical material. The widest range of reference is found in that founding text of modern economics *The Wealth of Nations*.[30] Smith offered historical examples to demonstrate how the development of the division of labor was limited by the accessibility of water transport and hence the size of the market that could be reached;[31] he cited Roman agronomists as evidence for the practice of horticulture and viticulture in southern Europe,[32] and commented on the management of state lands by classical states;[33] he drew on Roman evidence to illustrate the relationship between supply and demand, showing that the price of luxuries in antiquity was not related to the low value of silver but to the abundance of labor and subsistence and hence the level of demand – a principle which is extrapolated to cover any society during the advancement of civilization.[34] The colonies of the Greeks and Romans offered, in his eyes, an excellent model for imitation: there were clear motives for their foundation, a clear basis for the relationship between colony and mother country, and a clear benefit for the latter, all of which stood in direct contrast to Britain's relationship with America.[35] Smith's analysis also encompassed subjects that would come to be excluded from economics: military affairs, in which the models for the superiority of a standing army over a militia were Macedon and Rome,[36] and education, where ancient evidence showed that "the demand for such education produced, what it always produces, the talent for giving it; and the emulation which an unrestrained competition never fails to excite appears to have brought the talent to a very high degree of perfection," without any need for state intervention.[37]

In the next generation, in the face of a new tendency within economic writing towards abstract and ahistorical generalization, Thomas Malthus would insist on the importance of drawing upon empirical evidence, especially historical material:

> The principal cause of error, and of the differences which prevail at present among the scientific writers on political economy, appears to me to be a precipitate attempt to simplify and generalise . . . [These writers] do not sufficiently try their theories by a reference to that enlarged and comprehensive experience which, on so complicated a subject, can alone establish their truth and utility.[38]

Malthus' approach to validating his "principle of population," the theory for which he is best known, rested on identifying its applicability to the whole range of historical societies: "that population has this constant tendency to increase beyond the means of subsistence, and that it is kept to its necessary level by these causes, will sufficiently appear from a review of the different states of society in which man has existed."[39] Successive editions of his *Essay on the Principle of Population* expanded the volume of historical material, with Book I, entitled "Of the checks to population in the less civilised parts of the world and in past times," including chapters on Greece and Rome and a detailed analysis of the demographic aspects of the fall of the Roman Republic.[40] Malthus placed considerable (and in the eyes of his opponents unacceptable) emphasis in his analysis on the role of personal "restraint" in controlling the urge to procreate and thus in limiting population growth, and made great play of the degree to which this varied between different cultures and so led to different historical outcomes. In his economic analysis he offered a similar account of variability in human motivation:

> It is extremely different in different countries and at different times in the same country. A day's labour of a Hindoo or a South-America Indian will not admit of a comparison with that of an Englishman . . . [Their response to a rise in wages] clearly shows how different may be the personal exertions of the labouring classes in the same country at different times; and how different therefore may be the products of a given number of days' labour, as the society proceeds from the indolence of the savage to the activity of the civilized state.[41]

Malthus presented this idea in terms of a simple dichotomy between the savage state and civilization – the former category apparently included

Poles and Irish day laborers – but the idea of variability in human behavior offered the obvious possibility of explaining modern European developments in terms of a contrast between the prevalent attitudes of different forms of "civilization," modern and pre-modern. While Smith tended to emphasize the comparability of different societies, Malthus was equally interested in historical difference, aiming to show that certain theories about the operations of the market were applicable only in specific conditions, above all dependent on the prevalent attitudes of the time.[42] A similar approach is found in the economic theories of James Steuart:

> I have already, upon several occasions, taken notice of the great difference between the political oeconomy of the antients, and that of modern times; for this reason, among others, that I perceive that the sentiments of the antients, which were founded upon reason and common sense, relative to their situation, have been adopted by some moderns, who have not perhaps sufficiently attended to the change of our manners, and to the effects which this change must operate upon every thing relative to our oeconomy.[43]

What these writers had in common, however, was an agreement on the importance of a broad, comparative approach to economic analysis, a commitment to the continuing relevance of classical examples and texts, and an absence of any conception that the modern world was fundamentally different in its economic constitution or uniformly superior in its qualities. Antiquity illuminated modernity – sometimes as a model, sometimes as a contrast – because they both represented different facets of a more general human experience.

History and Economics

There is a striking contrast between the range of historical allusions and references in eighteenth-century works like *The Wealth of Nations* and the paucity of such references in the writings of the next generation of economists, of theorists like David Ricardo. This reflects a significant shift in the way that the discipline of "political economy" came to be practiced and defined: increasingly abstract and deductive, aiming to identify economic laws and structures on the basis of logical principles, rather than deriving them from empirical evidence (precisely the tendency against which Malthus was arguing) and narrowing the scope of investigation to concentrate on purely "economic" matters rather than the broad-based

"Science of Man," combining economics, history, and moral philosophy, pursued by Smith.[44] Nineteenth-century economists made great claims for the utility of this new approach to understanding society, and founded these in part on an explicit rejection of alternative approaches. Historical evidence, it was suggested, offered only an unedifying mass of detail and precedent, which obscured the principles and forces that actually operated within the apparent chaos of the economy. As Ricardo argued against Malthus, "there are so many combinations, so many operating causes in Political Economy, that there is a great danger in appealing to experience in favour of a particular doctrine, unless we are sure that all the causes of variation are seen and their effects duly estimated."[45] History, according to the French economist Jean-Baptiste Say, presented merely a "sad spectacle" of violence, barbarism, and ignorance; "only political economy makes known the true ties that bind men in society. While discrediting old institutions it brings new force to good laws and good jurisprudence."[46]

Classical antiquity was thus excluded from serious consideration, along with all other historical material. Some of these writers occasionally touched on classical examples as a means of demonstrating the superiority of modern economic knowledge, which enabled the economist to understand the past better than any of its inhabitants or any mere historian. Jean-Baptiste Say offered a lengthy digression on the real value of Roman coinage, while Thomas de Quincey asserted that economic theory alone allowed a proper understanding of a passage of Theophrastus: "the case illustrates powerfully the uselessness of mere erudition in contending with a difficulty seated in the matter – substantially in the thing – and not in the Greek or Latin expression. Here, in Theophrastus, it was not Greek, it was political economy, that could put it to rights."[47] There is a hint of resentment in some of these authors, even a century later, that the classics continued to excite any interest at all; the great Alfred Marshall felt it worth complaining that the low status of economics in academic circles might be due to the influence of the classical Greeks' dismissive attitude towards business.[48] In general, however, the subject was simply ignored. If the past was to be considered at all in a survey of the origins of the modern economy or of modern economic thought, classical antiquity, which had produced scarcely any examples of abstract economic thought worth engaging with (Aristotle might still be claimed as a pioneer of rudimentary economic analysis), had little to offer.[49] As Say put it, the writings of the ancients proclaimed "their utter ignorance of the nature and origin of wealth, of the manner in which it is distributed and of the effects of its consumption."[50]

What is also missing from these writers, however, is any articulation or discussion of the nature of modernity from an economic standpoint. Remarkably, the economic tradition moved from the failure of Smith and his contemporaries to recognize the full extent and implications of how society was being transformed to the apparent tendency in their successors to take this transformation entirely for granted. There is some acknowledgment, at least in the economic writings of John Stuart Mill, that the growth of industry and the application of technology had given present-day society a significant advantage over earlier periods, reflected not least in the scale of activity: "at what period were the operations of productive industry carried on upon anything like their present scale? Were so many hands ever before employed at the same time upon the same work, as now in all the principal departments of manufactures and commerce?"[51] Though it seems rather half-hearted in comparison to Marx's encomium of modernity, Mill articulated a clear sense of pride and superiority in the modern world's achievements, particularly emphasizing that this had been achieved despite the abolition of slavery:

> Without compulsory labour an enormous mass of food is annually extracted from the soil, and maintains, besides the actual producers, an equal, sometimes greater number of labourers, occupied in producing conveniences and luxuries of innumerable kinds, or in transporting them from place to place; also a multitude of persons employed in directing and superintending these various labours; and over and above all these, a class more numerous than in the most luxurious ancient societies of persons whose occupations are of a kind not directly productive, and of persons who have no occupation at all. The food thus raised supports a far larger population than had ever existed (at least in the same regions) on an equal space of ground, and supports them with certainty. Besides this great increase in the quantity of food, it has greatly improved in quality and variety; while conveniences and luxuries . . . descend, in great abundance, through many widening strata in society.[52]

However, there is little sign of an attempt, in Mill or other mainstream economic writers, at analyzing the roots of these changes or attempting to explore the nature of modernity in more detail. The key characteristics of the modern economy – industry rather than agriculture, advancing technology, a largely free market, widespread availability of credit, a society open to the values of industry, and the advice of economists – were taken as a given, the basis for feelings of superiority over less developed societies but not, as one might have expected, the source of crucial questions about the nature of economic development or the significance of historical variation in economic structures.[53]

The explanation for this neglect clearly lies in the assumption, shared by all the writers within this tradition, that the principles and laws which they identified as determining the operations of the economy were universally applicable, and would – if one took the trouble – be easily identifiable in any past historical context. As Say put it, in a discussion of the true causes of the famine that took place in Antioch in 363 CE, "the principles of political economy are eternal and immutable; but one nation is acquainted with them, and another not."[54]

> The maxims of political economy are immutable; ere yet observed and discovered, they were operating in the way above described; the same cause regularly produced the same effect; the wealth of Tyre and of Amsterdam originated in a common source. It is society that has been subject to change, in the progressive advancement of industry.[55]

The past was ignored not because it was felt to be wholly different and hence irrelevant to the understanding of present-day economic structures, but because it was seen to be, at bottom, essentially similar. Historical analysis would at best add nothing to attempts at understanding the economy, and at worst produce confusion by creating the appearance of differences and inconsistencies and suggesting that clear, logically derived economic principles should be rejected in favor of policies based on a superficial understanding of local, contingent circumstances. In brief, modernity did not need to be defined or analyzed – indeed, the concept might be considered redundant – because the principles of political economy applied to "the economy" as a universal phenomenon.

The Failure of Antiquity

There were exceptions to the anti-historical turn in economic studies in the nineteenth century. In England, the pioneering economic historian Arnold Toynbee lamented the fact that Smith's example had not been followed by his successors and that "the form of modern text-books is due to Ricardo, whose mind was entirely unhistorical."[56] He argued instead for the "historical method" as something approaching pure inductivism: "not only does it investigate the stages of economic development in a given country, but it compares them with those which have obtained in other countries and times, and seeks by comparison to discover laws of universal application."[57] In Germany, writers like Wilhelm Roscher and Friedrich List, often considered to constitute a coherent "German historical school" in economic thought, offered similar arguments, insisting on the need for economists to study the past above all because of its variation and difference from the present.[58] "The student of public economy must familiarize himself," declared Roscher, the self-proclaimed Thucydides of political economy, "with the variations that have taken place in what men, at different periods of history, have required of the state and public economy, until he is lost in wonder at the contemplation."[59] Indeed, the variation and mutability of economic institutions should be regarded as a human necessity rather than an evil. List, meanwhile, drew support from the past, above all from the example of classical Athens, for his insistence on the importance of political freedom for economic progress – "history contains no record of a rich, commercial and industrial community that was not at the same time in the enjoyment of freedom"[60] – but also for an ironic critique of the changing status of – for the present time – apparently incontrovertible economic doctrines such as free trade.[61] These ideas influenced economic historians like Karl Bücher: "an historically constructive view, such as we will here present, must from the start shake off the idea that any particular form in any department of economic activity can be the norm for all times and people."[62]

Roscher and List echoed the early political economists, above all Adam Smith, not only in their emphasis on the importance of a historical perspective but in their understanding of the character of modernity: the high development of the division of labor – Roscher illustrated its importance by contrasting it with the Homeric examples of Penelope working at the loom, Nausicaa working as a laundress, and Odysseus acting as a carpenter[63] – and a familiar miscellany of other factors: "We are approaching more nearly to [a world economy] by the ways of the more and more cosmopolitan character of science, the increasing international cooperation of labour, the improvement in the means of transportation, growing emigration, the greater love of peace, and the greater toleration of nations."[64] In place of Smith's division of world history into pastoral, agricultural, and commercial societies, Roscher and Bücher focused on the degree of organization of economic activity, with the present characterized by the emergence of a world economy out of the earlier stages of family or household, municipal, and national economies. "In the course of history mankind sets before itself ever higher economic aims and finds the means of attaining these in a division of labour, which constantly extends until finally it embraces the whole people and requires the services of all for all."[65] Like Smith's schema, this framework did not exclude the possibility that pre-modern societies might already have reached the higher levels of development. While Bücher himself considered that most of classical antiquity was dominated by the household or *oikos* economy, and provoked a furious response from ancient historians as a result,[66] Roscher and List characterized the classical Greek cities and especially the Roman Empire in much more positive terms. Further, they remained happy to draw analogies between past and present, as well as contrasts. In the context of the "Social Question" that dominated their discussions, namely the consideration of the social impact of modernity and in particular the unemployment, poverty, and inequality that seemed to be the unavoidable result of economic transformation, the history of Rome came to be seen as a vital example of the consequences of too divergent economic interests.[67] These ideas also found expression in ancient history in the work of Theodor Mommsen, who identified economic factors as a crucial element in the fall of the Republic – "in consequence of the one-sided prominence assigned to capital in the Roman economy, the evils inseparable from a pure capitalist system could not fail to appear"[68] – and who insisted on the need "to bring the ancients down from the fantastic pedestal on which they appear into the real world. That is why the consul had to become the Bürgermeister."[69] Once again, the economic differences between antiquity and modernity were blurred to the extent that each could, in theory, shed light on the other.

The most important heir of this "Historical School," however, took a different approach. For Max Weber, the nature and origins of capitalism were the central concern of his life's work, and he placed the question of the differences between modern and pre-modern societies, especially classical antiquity, at the heart of his account.[70] This choice might be attributed to Weber's background in ancient history – his *Habilitationsschrift* (advanced doctoral dissertation) considered the relation between Roman agrarian history and the development of Roman law – but there was also a strong methodological argument in its favor.[71] The comparative method offered the opportunity both of characterizing modernity more precisely and of testing different theories of economic development. Ancient and medieval societies were in significant respects similar, and sufficiently different from other (non-European) societies such as China, above all in their degree of legal sophistication, urbanization, and rational thought; comparisons of ancient and medieval economic structures could then clarify the reasons why one society had been the birthplace of modernity and the other had not. Discussing the possibility of producing a comparative study of the ancient and medieval city, Weber remarked:

> Of course, I say this on the assumption that such a comparative study would not aim at finding "analogies" and "parallels" . . . The aim should, rather, be precisely the opposite: to identify and define the individuality of each development, the characteristics which made the one conclude in a manner so different from the other. This done, one can then determine the causes which led to these differences.[72]

Weber's characterization of modernity began with the conventional list of familiar features: large-scale industry, the application of technology, free labor, state policies favorable to profitable activity. "The industrial capitalism of antiquity led to virtually no improvement, as compared to craft work, in the technology and organisation of production . . . Today capital has enlisted science in its service and uses it to develop large units of production with internal division of labour and concomitant technology."[73] Although he observed that "occasionally in antiquity there were approaches towards rationalized, large-scale production," it was generally accepted that economic specialization was a limited and atypical phenomenon in the ancient world.[74] In contrast to more narrowly "economic" writers, he also emphasized the role of the law in setting the conditions under which economic activity took place: "the specific characteristics of modern capitalist development, industrial capitalism, is based on legal institutions which were created in the medieval industrial cities, institutions which did not exist in the ancient polis."[75] Joint liability enterprises, legal institutions, and the modern system of money and credit were noted as essential components of western capitalism, alongside larger factories, division of labor, specialization of production, and the development of mass disposable income.[76]

Above all, however, Weber emphasized social and psychological aspects – the vital importance of a distinctively modern approach to economic activity and to life in general in bringing new institutions and forms of behavior into being. Earlier writers on the economy had tended to follow Hume's assumptions about the continuity of human nature:

> Would you know the sentiments, inclinations and course of life of the Greeks and Romans? Study well the temper and the actions of the French and English . . . Mankind are so much the same, in all times and places, that history informs us of nothing new or strange in this particular.[77]

If the Greeks and Romans are like the modern English, then the reverse is also true, and so differences in sentiments or attitudes can scarcely explain differences in economic structure or performance. James Steuart argued that "man we find acting uniformly in all ages, in all countries and in all climates, from the principles of self-interest, expediency, duty or passion," and Adam Smith's statement about the willingness of those who possess a surplus to exchange it, was similarly presented as an eternal truism.[78] The likes of Malthus and Roscher referred to differences in customs and attitudes, but not to a fundamental distinction in mentality or motivation. In Weber's account, however, the development of capitalism is linked explicitly to a modern mentality that is not found, or at best found only in an undeveloped, restricted form, in earlier societies; it is not mere acquisitiveness – "this impulse exists and has existed among waiters, physicians, coachmen, artists, prostitutes, dishonest officials, soldiers, nobles, crusaders, gamblers, and beggars. One may say that it has been common to all sorts and conditions of men at all times and in all countries of the earth" – but the rational pursuit of forever renewed profit, forgoing immediate gratification for the sake of future returns.[79] The rise of the modern economy is to be explained by a "specifically Occidental bourgeois mentality," which then shaped the entire development.[80]

Weber argued for the existence of a form of capitalism in antiquity: "Where we find that property is an object of trade and is utilised by individuals for profit-making enterprise in a market economy, there we have capitalism. If this be accepted, then it becomes perfectly clear that capitalism shaped whole periods of Antiquity, and indeed precisely those periods we call 'golden ages.'"[81] Unlike non-European societies, which simply lacked the necessary mental equipment to support such a development, classical antiquity had had the potential to become the direct source of modernity. The question was then why this capitalism had failed to establish itself as the ruling principle of ancient society, and so failed to support or promote economic development along modern lines. The answer, in Weber's view, had to be sought in the context within which economic agents operated, the social and cultural institutions of antiquity.

> When the Mediterranean world was unified and pacified in the Hellenistic period and then under the Roman Empire, the ancient city became the centre of exclusively economic interests. As a result the trade associations of merchants and artisans, previously present only in elementary form, began to develop and flourish. They were used by the Roman Empire for its own purposes, and we can follow their further development down to the beginnings of the medieval guilds. But the death-knell of ancient capitalism had sounded long before; the new peace and the monarchical state, the shift of society's centre from the coasts to the hinterland – all these changes throttled ancient capitalism instead of causing it to flourish (as one might *a priori* expect).[82]

Capitalism Ancient and Modern

It is perfectly possible to regard the ahistorical turn in mainstream economics in the nineteenth century as an innocent mistake or as the result of the preference on the part of an influential figure like Ricardo for abstraction over detail – or, as Bücher seems to imply, as part of a general tendency on the part of the moderns: "civilised man has always had a great inclination to read his conceptions and feelings into the mind of primitive man; but he has only a limited capacity for understanding the latter's undeveloped mental life and for interpreting, as it were, his nature."[83] A very different perspective was offered by Karl Marx, another heir of Adam Smith's vision of a broad-based and historically aware "Science of Man," who regarded the presuppositions of contemporary political economy as anything but innocent.[84] By neglecting history, Marx argued, economists were able to ignore the fundamental differences between modernity and all that had gone before, and to regard the past – insofar as they noted it at all – as either an underdeveloped version of the present or as an aberration from the "natural" forms of the present day.[85] "Economists express the relations of bourgeois production, the division of labour, credit, money etc. as fixed, immutable, eternal categories."[86] Such categories of thought may be considered adequate for describing the economy of the present, but since they take its essential features for granted, rather than exploring the question of how they had come to develop out of different forms of economic activity, they are incapable of providing a full understanding of its underlying logic. In other words, they are insufficient for a full understanding of the structure and dynamics of the modern economy. In a historically informed perspective, on the other hand, "all the mystery of the world of commodities, all the magic and necromancy that shrouds labour-products in the context of commodity production in smoke, vanishes as soon as we flee to other forms of production."[87]

Not only did modern economists believe, mistakenly, that their theories were sufficient for understanding the modern economy, they considered them to have universal validity. Marx was willing to concede that, since the modern economy had developed out of earlier forms, modern categories of analysis could offer useful insights into those earlier forms – but only if their essential differences were also kept in mind.[88] It is always possible to describe non-modern economic activities in modern terms, but this can never be an innocent procedure: "this is a very convenient method by which to demonstrate the eternal validity of the capitalist mode of production and to regard capital as an immutable natural element in human production as such."[89]

> The materials and means of labour, a proportion of which consists of the products of previous work, play their part in every labour process in every age and in all circumstances. If, therefore, I label them "capital" in the confident knowledge that "semper aliquid haeret," then I have proved that the existence of capital is an eternal law of nature of human production and that the Xinghiz who cuts down rushes with a knife he has stolen from a Russian so as to weave them together to make a canoe is just as true a capitalist as Herr von Rothschild. I could prove with equal facility that the Greeks and Romans celebrated communion because they drank wine and ate bread.[90]

By regarding its provisional, historically specific categories of thought as expressing universal human nature, by ignoring the past or treating it simply as a watered-down or less developed version of the present, economic theory sought to establish "*bourgeois* relations" as "the inviolable laws on which society in the abstract is founded. This is more or less the conscious purpose of the whole proceeding."[91] Economists stand therefore as the defenders of the status quo against revolutionary ideas of how society might be reconstituted on a more just and equal basis. Describing pre-modern societies in modern terms is not merely the product of a limited perspective and understanding, it is expressly intended to suggest the futility of struggling against present social and economic conditions, since these are presented as the natural outcomes of human nature.

In contrast, Marx looked to the past for two essential interconnected purposes. The first was to gain an understanding of the material basis of human existence, and hence a set of tools for analyzing the economic structures of any given society; the second was to identify the "laws of motion" of economic development on the world-historical scale, and hence to chart the future development of modern capitalism. The theme of historical difference, presenting human history in terms of a succession of distinct "modes of production," was essential for both of these purposes: it demonstrated the inadequacy of "bourgeois" economics, with its illegitimate assumption of universality and timelessness, as a framework for full understanding, and it established that capitalism was not an eternal law of human nature. As capitalism had clearly not always existed, there was no reason to suppose that it would last for ever.

> In broad outline, the Asiatic, ancient, feudal and modern bourgeois modes of production may be designated as epochs marking progress in the economic development of society. The bourgeois relations of production are the last antagonistic form of the social process of production – antagonistic not in the sense of individual antagonism but of an antagonism that emanates from the individuals' social conditions of existence – but the productive forces developing within bourgeois society create also the material conditions for a solution of this antagonism.[92]

Within this analytical framework, the nature of the economic organization of classical antiquity was of central importance. If this sophisticated society had been organized around principles other than those of capitalism, this constituted the clearest possible proof that Marx's insights were to be preferred to those of the economists who saw capitalism everywhere. And not only economists; Marx was equally scathing about ancient historians, and especially the influential Mommsen, who insisted on adopting the terminology of modern economics in their accounts of the past:

> In encyclopedias of classical antiquity one can read such absurdities as that in the ancient world capital was fully developed "except that the free worker and the credit-system were lacking." Herr Mommsen too, in his History of Rome, commits one "Quidproquo" after another.[93]

Even in those agricultural economies of ancient times which show most analogy with the capitalist rural economy, Carthage and Rome, the similarity is more with the plantation economy than with the form truly corresponding to the capitalist mode of exploitation. A formal analogy, which however appears as a complete delusion in all essential points to anyone who has understood the capitalist mode of production, even if not for someone like Herr Mommsen, who discovers the capitalist mode of production in every monetary economy – such a formal analogy is to be found nowhere in mainland Italy in ancient times, but only to some extent in Sicily, because this existed as the agricultural tributary for Rome . . . Here we find leaseholders in a modern sense.[94]

In his analysis, as discussed at the beginning of this chapter, Marx identified the whole range of features that distinguished the modern economy from its predecessors: division of labor, application of technology, expansion of trade and markets, growth of credit and money. Anticipating some of Weber's arguments, he emphasized the existence of differences in the values and the economic mentality of the ancients: "Wealth does not appear as the aim of production . . . The question is always which mode of property creates the best citizens."[95]

Money is itself a commodity, an external object, which can become the private property of anyone. The social power thus becomes the private power of private persons. Ancient society therefore denounced it as the coinage of division[96] of their economic and moral order. Modern society, which already in its infancy hauls Plutus by his hair out of the bowels of the earth, greets in the gold-grail the glittering incarnation of its innermost principle of life.[97]

However, none of these factors constituted the absolute distinction between past and present, none implied a decisive break in continuity between pre-modern and modern. Underlying all of them, Marx argued, were differences in the way that labor was organized and exploited. Capitalism, the "mode of production" that constituted and shaped modernity, was defined by the exploitation of free labor by the owners of capital, who thereby benefited from the willingness of free men to work harder to improve their position. Classical antiquity, in contrast, was based on the exploitation of slaves.

The sporadic application of co-operation on a large scale in the ancient world, in the Middle Ages, and in modern colonies, rests on unmediated relationships of domination and subjugation, in most cases on slavery. The capitalist form in contrast presupposes from the beginning the free wage-labourer, who sells his labour-power to capital.[98]

This approach clearly drew on the arguments of earlier political economists about the economic role of slavery. However, whereas many of them regarded slavery as an unfortunate aberration or moral failing by the Greeks, Marx followed the philosopher G. W. F. Hegel, one of the most important influences on his early work, in seeing it as one of the fundamental organizing principles of antiquity.[99] Slavery was not simply an institution, if that implies that it might have been abolished or modified with little effect on the rest of ancient society; on the contrary, slavery shaped the entire world view of the ancients. This in turn explains their different attitudes to wealth and production, as well as Aristotle's failure to grasp the true origin of value as the product of labor – in other words, it accounts for antiquity's intellectual as well as material underdevelopment.

Classical antiquity was the indirect source of modernity; it gave birth to feudalism through the same process of contradiction and conflict that later created capitalism out of feudalism and would in due course overcome capitalism in its turn.

> We have seen therefore that the means of production and exchange, on the basis of which the bourgeoisie built itself up, were created in feudal society. At a certain stage in the development of these means of production and exchange, the relations whereby feudal society produced and exchanged, the feudal organisation of agriculture and manufacturing, in a word the feudal property-relations, no longer corresponded to the already-developed forces of production. They were transformed into so many fetters. They had to be broken; they were broken.[100]

Antiquity, like feudalism, was a stage that had to be overcome in order to allow the creative and productive potential of human labor to develop further, rather than being held back by the material and cultural limitations of slavery. At the same time, however, classical antiquity pointed to the future, showing the necessity of overthrowing capitalism and seeking to build a new form of modernity that would not rest on any form of exploitation. There was little argument that the augmentation of human capacities and their liberation from the constraints of nature as a result of the modern economic transformation was, at least in principle, a positive development. However, for Marx these necessary advances came at an unacceptable cost:

> On the one hand, there have started into life industrial and scientific forces, which no epoch of the former human history had ever suspected. On the other hand, there exist symptoms of decay, far surpassing the horrors recorded of the latter times of the Roman Empire. In our days, everything seems pregnant with its contrary. Machinery, gifted with the wonderful power of shortening and fructifying human labour, we behold starving and overworking it. The new-fangled sources of wealth, by some strange weird spell, are turned into sources of want. The victories of art seem bought by the loss of character. At the same pace that mankind masters nature, man seems to become enslaved to other men or to his own infamy. Even the pure light of science seems unable to shine but on the dark background of ignorance. All our invention and progress seem to result in endowing material forces with intellectual life, and in stultifying human life into a material force.[101]

Comparison with the past revealed the deficiencies and failures of modernity; not only had it failed to live up to its own promises, it had failed to surpass societies over which it claimed superiority, and had even fallen short of their achievements. Slavery continued, in practice if not in legal form; starvation and want had not been banished; ignorance still ruled. Capitalism had produced wonders surpassing pyramids, aqueducts, and cathedrals; Marx does not name them, partly because this is unnecessary – every facet of modern civilization, not merely a few of its products, vastly exceeds the greatest monuments of past ages – but also because there is no point, as they will imminently be torn down and replaced. Modernity can easily surpass the past in scale and spectacle, but not in duration; it builds nothing to last, and its throwaway monuments to profit and exploitation encapsulate the spirit of its culture, just as temples and aqueducts had done for the Greeks and Romans. The enduring legacy of classical antiquity, the ultimate source of so many of modernity's professed ideals, stands as a reproach, a permanent reminder of why a further revolutionary transformation in society is required. However, it also represents a source of hope, as its existence demonstrates the possibility that a sophisticated society could be founded on quite different principles of economic and social organization. This was why, for Marx, the consul should *not* become the Bürgermeister, and the absolute distinction between ancient and modern should be constantly reiterated, but nevertheless the society and culture of the classical world remained at the heart of his economic analysis of modernity.

Notes

1   See generally Berman (1982), 87–129.
2   *Manifest der Kommunistischen Partei*, 466.
3   Ibid., 465.
4   Ibid., 467.
5   Cf. Goody (2004).
6   The phrase comes from Karl Polanyi (1944).
7   See generally Winch (1996).
8   Sekora (1977); Berry (1994).
9   Winch (1996), 80–7.
10 E.g. Wallace, *Dissertation on the Numbers of Mankind*.
11 Voltaire, *Philosophical Dictionary*, 290–2.
12 Hume, "Of refinement in the arts," 305.
13 Smith, *Wealth of Nations*, V.ii.k.3.
14 Hume, "On the populousness of antient nations," 410.
15 Ibid., 412.
16 Steuart, *Inquiry into the Principles of Political Oeconomy*, I, 428.
17 Ibid., II, 139–40.
18 Smith, *Wealth of Nations*, I.x.c.62; IV.ix.47.
19 Saint-Simon, "Of the industrial system," II.1.
20 Smith, *Wealth of Nations*, III.ii.9.
21 Mill, "Grote's History of Greece II," 315; generally, Finley (1980).
22 *Wealth of Nations*, I.i.1.
23 Ibid., I.i.11.
24 Ibid., I.ii.1.
25 Wrigley (1987); Coleman (1992), 1–42.
26 Steuart, *Inquiry into the Principles of Political* Oeconomy, II, 273.
27 *Wealth of Nations*, III.i.9.
28 Ibid., I.ix.e.15; I.xi.m.10–11.
29 Skinner (1975).
30 See generally Coleman (1987), 5–18.
31 *Wealth of Nations*, I.iii.4–6.
32 Ibid., I.xi.b.26.
33 Ibid., V.ii.a.13–14.
34 Ibid., I.xi.k.1.
35 Ibid., IV.vii.a–b.
36 Ibid., V.i.a.

37 Ibid., V.i.f.
38 Malthus, *Principles of Political Economy*, 4–5.
39 Malthus, *Essay on the Principle of Population*, 6–7.
40 Ibid., 112–24; Winch (1996), 305, 365, 369.
41 *Principles of Political Economy*, 283.
42 Ibid., 213, 355.
43 *Inquiry into the Principles of Political Oeconomy*, I, 167.
44 Collini, Winch, and Burrow (1983), 63–89; Kadish (1989); Hodgson (2001), esp. 3–32.
45 *Works*, 295.
46 Say, "On the influence," 149.
47 Say, *Treatise on Political Economy*, 248–54; de Quincey, *Logic of Political Economy*, 243.
48 Marshall, *Principles of Economics*, 729.
49 Cf. Meikle (1995) on Aristotle's "economics" and its reception.
50 *Treatise on Political Economy*, xxviii.
51 Mill, "Civilization," 125.
52 Mill, *Principles of Political Economy*, I, 23.
53 Cf. Hodgson (2001).
54 *Treatise on Political Economy*, 194 note.
55 Ibid., 340.
56 *Lectures on the Industrial Revolution*, 2.
57 Ibid., 4; cf. Hodgson (2001), 75–6.
58 Grimmer-Solem (2003).
59 *Principles of Political Economy*, I, 107.
60 *National System of Political Economy*, 109.
61 Ibid., 16.
62 *Entstehung der Volkswirtschaft*, 152.
63 *Principles of Political Economy*, I, 187.
64 Ibid., 80.
65 Bücher, *Entstehung der Volkswirtschaft*, 141.
66 Pearson (1957); relevant texts in Finley (1979).
67 Grimmer-Solem (2003), 89–126.
68 *History of Rome*, II, 386.
69 Letter to from Mommsen to Herzen, quoted in Gooch (1920), 457.
70 Bottomore (1985), 22–34; Love (1991).
71 Käsler (1988), 24–32.
72 *Agrarian Sociology of Ancient Civilizations*, 385.
73 Ibid., 207–8.
74 Ibid., 356.
75 Ibid., 339–40.
76 *Economy and Society*, I, 165–6; *Agrarian Sociology of Ancient Civilizations*, 354–8.

77 *Enquiries Concerning Human Understanding*, 83.
78 Steuart, *Inquiry into the Principles of Political Oeconomy*, I, 7; Smith, *Wealth of Nations*, I.xi.c.7.
79 *Protestant Ethic and the Spirit of Capitalism*, 17.
80 "The Protestant sects and the spirit of capitalism."
81 *Agrarian Sociology of Ancient Civilizations*, 50–1.
82 Ibid., 358.
83 *Entstehung der Volkswirtschaft*, 3.
84 McCarthy (1990), 209–46, on Marx's critique of Ricardo.
85 *Poverty of Philosophy*, 120–1.
86 Ibid., 104.
87 *Kapital*, I, 90.
88 *Grundrisse*, 105–6.
89 *Results of the Intermediate Process of Production*, 998.
90 Ibid., 998–9.
91 *Grundrisse*, 87.
92 *Contribution to the Critique of Political Economy*, 263–4.
93 *Kapital*, I, 182 n.39.
94 *Kapital*, III, 795.
95 *Grundrisse*, 487.
96 *Scheidemünze*, which conventionally refers to fractional coinage.
97 *Kapital*, I, 146–7.
98 Ibid., 354.
99 Finley (1980), 40–1.
100 *Manifest der Kommunistischen Partei*, 467.
101 Marx, Speech at the Anniversary of the *People's Paper*.

3

Before Alienation

The Classical Critique
of Modern Society

Man depicts himself in his actions, and what an image he presents in the
drama of the present time! Here a return to wildness, there lethargy: the
two extremes of human decline, and both combined in a single period.

F. Schiller, *Über der ästhetische Erziehung des Menschen* 5.3

"We are in an entirely new condition of society," declared the Swiss
historian and economist Jean Simonde de Sismondi in 1819.[1] A few years
later the French philosopher Auguste Comte emphasized the homogeneity
of all previous social forms in comparison to contemporary "Industrial
Society": "all the varieties of social organisation which have hitherto existed,
have only been modifications more or less extensive of a single system,
the Military and Theological system."[2] Meanwhile another French theor-
ist, the Comte de Saint-Simon, talked of a "complete change in the social
system," which represented "the passage from a feudal ecclesiastical
system to an industrial and scientific one."[3] Earlier generations of
Enlightenment thinkers had been inspired by the idea that a new form
of society, built on the principles of reason and justice, might be looked
for in the future, brought into being through the actions of reformers.[4]
By the early nineteenth century, at least in part as a result of the
perceived excesses and failings of the French Revolution, this view was
increasingly replaced by skepticism about the utility of utopian speculation on social issues – "there is a *nature of things* that does not depend
on human will, and which we cannot arrange according to our own wishes,"
as the economist Jean-Baptiste Say argued.[5] However, in many commentators this came hand in hand with the belief that a new form of
society, radically different from that of earlier periods, had already

arisen, quite spontaneously, as a natural consequence of the progress of "civilization."

> Civilisation properly so called consists on one hand in the development of the human mind, on the other in the result of this, namely the increasing power of man over nature . . . It is easy to perceive that the state of the social organisation essentially depends on that of civilisation and should be regarded as its result.[6]

In many respects, the development of interpretations of modernity as a social phenomenon closely followed that of the economic perspective. Like the political economists, the nineteenth-century founders of the scientific study of modern society looked to the past to emphasize the special nature both of their object of analysis and of their own approach to understanding it:

> Having reached the highest vantage point on the road to civilisation, the philosopher will discern, on the one hand, the remotest past, and, on the other, the most distant future; he will see in the background of the picture the establishment of slavery . . . The philosopher will go on to consider, with lively satisfaction, and looking at that part of the road leading to the place where he is now standing, the diminution of slavery, the progress of enlightenment, the gradual improvement of the human race, and, lastly, in the state of the French nation, which today forms its *avant-garde*, the complete abolition of slavery and a readiness to accept a social organisation which has the good of the majority as its primary object.[7]

However, this degree of self-satisfaction and optimism about the present state of society was relatively rare. Whereas the economic achievements of modernity, and its absolute superiority to earlier societies, were often celebrated without reservation, consideration of modern social and political issues tended to produce a more equivocal response. If the new society had indeed arrived, it was necessary to explain its failure as yet to live up to the expectations raised by the utopian speculations of the eighteenth century, and above all to account for the failure both of the French Revolution and of all attempts at restoring social stability in its aftermath. Saint-Simon's investigation of the origins and nature of the "industrial system" was presented as a response to decades of political crisis in France, understood by governments and governed alike "only in a vague and incomplete way," resulting from the still incomplete transformation of society.[8]

Comte, too, perceived "a movement of disorganisation," through which "society is hurried towards a profound moral and political anarchy which appears to menace it with a near and inevitable dissolution," as one of the defining features of the present epoch, a direct result of the fact that a fully modern social system had not yet entirely replaced its declining predecessor.[9]

Comparison with the past could emphasize the special nature and achievements of modern society, but it could also raise questions about why the modern world had not achieved more. As John Stuart Mill noted, "with all the advantages of this age, its facilities for mental cultivation, the incitements and rewards which it holds out to exalted talents, there can scarcely be pointed out in the European annals any stirring times which have brought so little that is distinguished, either morally or intellectually, to the surface."[10] Ten years later he remained unpersuaded of the absolute superiority of the present day over classical Greece. On the one hand, "their institutions, their way of life, even that which is their greatest distinction, the cast of their sentiments and development of their faculties, were radically inferior to the best (we wish it could be said to the collective) products of modern civilization."[11] On the other hand,

> To disparage what mankind owes to Greece, because she has not left for their imitation a perfect type of human character, nor a highly improved pattern of social institutions, would be to demand from the early youth of the human race what is far from being yet realized in its more advanced age. It would better become us to consider whether we have, in these particulars, advanced as much beyond the best Grecian model, as might with reason have been expected after more than twenty centuries.[12]

Those who believed in the potential of modern society needed faith that its full achievement was yet to be realized, so that current failings could be attributed to its immaturity or incomplete ascendancy over traditional structures. The modern economy, as even its critics fully conceded, was demonstrably superior to its predecessors; modern society was clearly distinct, but comparison with the past did not, as yet, work entirely in its favor.

For many commentators, indeed, the confrontation of past and present revealed not merely the underperformance of the latter but its inadequacy, inhumanity, and failure. In the middle of the eighteenth century, contemplation of history had revealed to Jean-Jacques Rousseau the inexorable decline of humanity as it fell away from the state of Nature:

In a word, he will explain how the human soul and passions, by imperceptible adulterations, so to speak change in Nature; why in the long run the objects of our needs and our pleasures change; why, as original man gradually vanishes, Society no longer offers to the wise man anything other than an assemblage of artificial men and factitious passions which are the products of all these new relationships, and have no foundation in nature.[13]

All civilization, not just modernity, represented for Rousseau an estrangement from nature and naturalness, the sole consolation for this development being the creation of opportunities for the exercise of virtue, "the soul's most delicate feeling," within society.[14] However, modern society could nevertheless be seen as a special case, in so far as the political institutions of earlier societies – above all, in Rousseau's view, Rome and Sparta – had not threatened man's humanity in the same way. Later writers followed Rousseau's lead in locating the source of modern discontent and social malaise not in the human condition itself but in the structures and institutions of contemporary society.[15] Further, "society" or "civilization" were henceforth considered as coherent wholes, and therefore susceptible to analysis in terms of their structures and organizing principles.[16] These two ideas then raised the possibility of, or at least the longing for, a complete transformation of social structures that would enable humanity to recover the qualities felt to have been lost in the transition to modernity.

Comparison with the past, and above all with the classical past, was central to these intellectual developments. Where Rousseau had often employed an idealized "state of nature" as a mirror for modern society, later writers focused almost exclusively on comparisons with other "states of civilization," as indicators of what modernity could have been. This accentuated their dissatisfaction with the modern by highlighting its perceived deficiencies and excesses – at the same time as it aggravated the long-standing tendency to idealize this past for its possession of superior qualities. The comparison demonstrated that an alternative was conceivable: modern institutions and customs were not universal but historically limited and specific to the present age. As Friedrich Schiller argued, in one of the most extensive and explicit comparisons of antiquity and modernity:

Have I perhaps in this description of the present time gone too far? I do not expect this objection, but another: that I have gone too far in my conclusions from it. This depiction, you will tell me, does indeed resemble present-day humanity, but it equally resembles all peoples which are caught up in civilisation . . . However, with more detailed consideration of the character of our time we will be left in astonishment at the contrast which is found between the present form of humanity and that of earlier times, especially the Greek. Our reputation for culture and refinement, which we rightly assert in comparison to any mere natural state, counts for nothing in comparison to Greek naturalness, which was wedded to all the charms of art and all the dignity of wisdom without – as is the case with us – being their victim. The Greeks put us to shame not just by a simplicity which is alien to our time; they are equally our rivals and often our models in the very same advantages with which we are in the habit of consoling ourselves for the unnaturalness of our manners. Equally full in form and content, both philosophical and creative, both sensitive and energetic, we see them combining the youthfulness of imagination with the maturity of reason in a glorious humanity.[17]

However, comparison with antiquity could do more than simply arouse, or confirm, feelings of dissatisfaction with the present state of things. It also offered a way of understanding the roots of the problems of modern society, if these could be attributed directly to the differences between ancient and modern social organization. The explanation for modern discontent must be either that we lack something which the Greeks (or, rarely but occasionally, the Romans) possessed, or that we have introduced damaging new institutions or practices from which they spared themselves. Finally, antiquity might be taken as a model for future developments, an alternative to the prospect of the indefinite continuation or intensification of present tendencies; or, if its recreation was regarded as impossible or undesirable, an ideal whose essential qualities would need to be reproduced at a higher stage in the future.

Scale, Complexity, and Specialization

There was little difficulty in identifying differences between ancient and modern society; accounts of classical history invariably had to spend some time explaining the particular nature of Greek or Roman social groups and their relation to one another, or the unusual workings of the Athenian or Roman Republican political systems. However, these differences were generally not seen as representing a fundamental separation between antiquity and modernity; on the contrary, the existence of social differentiation and political organization established both as belonging to the category of "civilization" rather than "savagery," and the differences between their systems were simply examples of the wide variety of ways in which human beings might organize themselves socially. The task of the historian was then to identify analogies or translations for classical social categories – "the *phyle* is the Roman tribe, and the *phratry* corresponds to the Roman curia, and to our own English *hundred*"[18] – or, more analytically, to identify the dominant principles of sociability (as for example George Grote in his *History of Greece* distinguished between religious and social aggregations and personal or local relationships in his analysis of Athenian social groups) from the range of possibilities known from modern society. The existence of social complexity carried more weight than the fact that ancient societies might be predominantly organized around relatively "primitive" forms of sociability like the clan.[19]

Conversely, attempts at developing general typologies of social groups or identifying the underlying principles of human social organization tended to assume that they would be, if not universally applicable, then at any rate applicable to classical society. In terms of the later development of the relevant academic disciplines, one might loosely say that, whereas economics separated itself from history altogether and focused solely on the modern, sociology took "complex society" as its field of enquiry, retaining a broad historical perspective and differentiating itself rather from anthropology as the study of the "primitive." Thus, although the definition of "class" in a Marxist sense, and hence its relevance for the analysis of Athenian or Roman society, remain fiercely contested issues within ancient history, it is clear from Marx and Engels' own references to the "class struggle" in ancient Rome – "freeman and slave, patrician and plebeian"[20] – that the term was intended to be almost universal.[21] "We find almost everywhere a complicated arrangement of society into various orders"; the task was then to demonstrate how this apparent variety of systems of social differentiation in fact concealed the same eternal opposition between oppressors and oppressed, determined by their relative positions in the system of production, and how, far from being a distinct social order which had done away with such antagonisms, modern bourgeois society simply presented a new, albeit simplified, version of them:

> [It] has not abolished class oppositions. It has only set up new classes, new conditions of oppression, new forms of struggle in place of the old. Our epoch, the epoch of the bourgeoisie, marks itself out, however, in this manner: it has simplified the class oppositions. Society as a whole is divided more and more into two great hostile camps, into two great classes, standing directly against one another: Bourgeoisie and Proletariat.[22]

The competing analytical concept of "status," elaborated by Max Weber, was not only presented as being applicable to a wide range of historical societies but was also delineated through the citation of evidence from many different cultural contexts, including classical antiquity.[23] Weber's argument shares the assumptions of Marx and Engels: the apparent variety of social forms in different historical contexts conceals the fact that they can be understood as manifestations of the same principles of social organization, common to modern and pre-modern societies.[24] In other words, differences in social terminology and in the specific criteria of membership of social groups can be regarded as relatively trivial; the different principles of ancient and modern social differentiation are considered to reflect, rather than to constitute, the incomparability of antiquity and modernity.

That is not to say that the theme of the special nature of modernity was not central to social analysis; rather, other differences between ancient and modern society were identified as establishing a fundamental distinction between them. The first of these was scale, already identified as a significant mark of difference in economic terms: the number and diversity of people in modern states and the size of the geographical area which had to be governed, which together raised the question of whether ancient forms of government and social organization could be at all compatible with the modern world. The German philosopher Hegel stated the issue bluntly: "given the size of modern states, it is quite impossible to realise the ideal of giving all free men a share in the discussion and resolution of universal political issues."[25] The ancient view that all citizens should participate in deliberations and discussions of state affairs, adopted as an ideal by many Enlightenment political theorists, clearly could not be realized in the same manner in the modern context: "Because our states are so large and the masses are so many, [the people] have to express their will in decisions on public affairs not directly but indirectly through representatives."[26]

Rousseau had noted that the idea of political representation was quite modern, and regarded this development as one of the fundamental flaws of modern society: it had replaced the true liberty of the ancients with a mute, passive, and self-serving liberty, in which the state did not embody the people's collective will but assumed their identity.[27] He attributed the decline of full and direct political participation not to practical constraints of scale but to human choice, citing historical examples with the aim of demonstrating that alternatives could exist even in a large and complex society:

The people assembled, it will be said! What a chimera! It is a chimera today, but it was not two thousand years ago. Have men changed in nature? The bounds of the possible in moral matters are less narrow than we think. It is our weaknesses, our vices, our prejudices that constrain them. Base souls do not believe in great men: vile slaves smirk mockingly at the word freedom. Let us consider what can be done in the light of what has been done; I shall not speak of the ancient republics of Greece, but the Roman Republic was, it seems to me, a large state, and the City of Rome a large city.[28]

However, this conclusion was not widely shared. Adam Smith, indeed, argued in response that the Roman Republic showed exactly why representative government was indispensable in a large, heterogeneous society. The enfranchisement of the Romans' Italian allies meant that Roman citizens were no longer known to one another, and so it became impossible to control who was participating in debates: "a rabble of any kind could be introduced into the assemblies of the people, could drive out the real citizens, and decide upon the affairs of the republick as if they themselves had been such."[29] Benjamin Constant echoed Rousseau's insistence on the different natures of ancient and modern liberty, conceding that the moderns had indeed lost something in the transition – "the individual, autonomous in his private life, is, even in states with the greatest liberty, sovereign only in appearance" – but sought to emphasize what had been gained as a result of the processes that had rendered representation indispensable:

> The exercise of political rights no longer affords us even a part of the joy which the ancients found in it; at the same time, the progress of civilisation, the commercial developments of the period and the communication of peoples with one another have multiplied and varied to infinity the means of individual pleasure.[30]

Clearly the different sizes of the political communities and their territories did not establish an absolute divide between ancient and modern, but for most commentators they established the incompatibility of modern society with one of the crucial institutions of classical Greece, the *polis*. As Hegel argued, "it is not hard to show that a state with all the citizens who as such have in their hands the supreme agency in all public affairs, can only be small and weak and must either be destroyed by itself or demolished from without in the course of world history."[31] If, as many writers believed, the *polis* represented some sort of ideal of political and social organization, it clearly could not be realized in modern society through the simple recreation of its institutions. Modern society was too large and insufficiently homogeneous; perhaps the Roman Empire, not the Republic, offered a better model:

> Diversity of language and dialect . . . and diversity of customs and cultures among the separate estates . . . Such heterogeneous and at the same time most powerful elements could be overcome and held together in the enlarged Roman Empire only by the weight of superior power, just as they are in modern states by the spirit and art of political organisation. Consequently, disparity of culture and customs has become a necessary product, as well as a necessary condition, of the continual existence of modern states.[32]

However, it was increasingly evident that modern society was not simply operating on a larger scale, it was infinitely more complex than earlier societies. Benjamin Constant bluntly described ancient republics as "limited."[33] Durkheim was among the writers who argued that the most important manifestation of this complexity, representing both the cause and the effect of the enormous variety of activities, goods, and pleasures now on offer in modern society, was the division and specialization of labor.[34]

> Though in a rude society there is a good deal of variety in the occupations of each individual, there is not a great deal in those of the whole society. Every man does, or is capable of doing, almost every thing which any other man does, or is capable of doing. Every man has a considerable degree of knowledge, ingenuity, and invention; but scarcely any man has a great degree. The degree, however, which is commonly possessed, is generally sufficient for conducting the whole simple business of the society. In a civilized state, on the contrary, though there is little variety in the occupations of the greater part of individuals, there is an almost infinite variety in those of the whole society.[35]

Indeed, in Adam Smith's view it was this variety that had brought into being the modern science of society, as contemplation of it rendered the understanding of those who had the leisure to think about such things "in an extraordinary degree, both acute and comprehensive." The division of labor was not of course confined to modernity; on the contrary, Smith's account of its early development focused on the history of ancient warfare as the clearest example of the beneficial link between specialization and technical progress.[36] John Stuart Mill, contemplating the history of "civilization," turned to the same theme to emphasize the power of "discipline" in social development: "discipline is more powerful than numbers, and discipline, that is, perfect co-operation, is an attribute of civilization."[37]

> The labourer in a rude state of society works singly, or if several are brought together by the will of a master, they work side by side, but not in concert: one man digs his piece of ground, another digs a similar piece of ground close by him. In the situation of an ignorant labourer, tilling even his own field with his own hands, and associating with no one except his wife and his children, what is there that can teach him to co-operate? The division of employment – the accomplishment by the combined labour of several, of tasks which could not be achieved by any number of persons singly – is the great school of co-operation.[38]

For Smith and Mill, history showed how specialization and cooperation were mutually reinforcing and constructive; they were not exclusive to the modern world but "the unexampled development which all these elements have assumed of late years" was the primary determinant of modernity's economic superiority over earlier societies.[39] Similar ideas can be found in Comte and, at the close of the nineteenth century, in Emile Durkheim's extensive study of *The Division of Labour in Society*: the division of labor to the extent that prevailed within modernity had produced an entire system of rights, duties, and mutual dependence, an exceptionally complex social system, in contrast to the restricted development and "mechanical" solidarity of earlier forms of society.[40]

One-Sided Development

However, compared with his predecessors, Durkheim's analysis of social complexity and the division of labor is in other respects remarkably pessimistic and skeptical. In his introduction, he emphasizes that, contrary to the perspective offered by the economists, the modern division of labor is not confined to production but encompasses every aspect of human society. More importantly, however, his aim is not simply to chart its inexorable progress but to consider the fundamental social question which it raises:

The development of man will be conceived in two entirely different ways, depending on whether we yield to the movement or resist it. At this point, an urgent question arises: Of these two directions, which must we choose? Is it our duty to seek to become a thorough and complete human being, one quite sufficient unto oneself; or, on the contrary, to be only a part of a whole, the organ of an organism? Briefly, is the division of labour, at the same time that it is a law of nature, also a moral rule of human conduct?[41]

This question can be addressed only through a historical perspective: Is it true that the happiness of the individual increases as man advances and society becomes more complex and interdependent? "Nothing is more doubtful."[42] Civilization was not developed in order to increase happiness (the past had no knowledge of the things which we now possess, and so no desire for them); rather, the division of labor has proceeded inexorably despite its negative effects on the lives of individuals. "It will be said that with civilised people life is more varied, and variety is necessary to pleasure. But at the same time as there is greater mobility, civilisation carries with it more uniformity, for it has imposed upon man monotonous and continuous labour."[43]

This analysis inherits a long tradition of criticism of the development of specialization as a distinctive feature of modern society. Its potential for increasing productive power and mastering nature was fully conceded by its opponents, who sought to judge it instead by its consequences for humanity and human beings. Specialization could equally well be described as the one-sided or restricted development of individuals, a process that produced what Max Weber described as "specialists without spirit, sensualists without heart," the "nullity" which believed it had reached the highest degree of civilization yet achieved.[44] The division of labor and the expansion of dependence and cooperation could just as easily be characterized as social fragmentation and a threat to individual freedom, in which people were condemned to predetermined roles within an intricate social machine.[45] Almost invariably, the basis for such arguments was comparison with the awesome and fully rounded humanity of the Greeks.

I do not underrate the advantages which the human race today, considered as a whole and weighed in the balance of intellect, can boast in the face of what is best in the ancient world. But it has to take up the challenge in serried ranks, and let whole measure itself against whole. What individual modern could sally forth and engage, man against man, with an individual Athenian for the prize of humanity? Whence this disadvantage among individuals when the species as a whole is at such an advantage? Why was the individual Greek qualified to be the representative of his age, and why can no single Modern venture as much? Because it was from all-unifying Nature that the former, and from the all-dividing intellect that the latter, received their respective forms. It was civilization itself which inflicted this wound upon modern man. Once the increase of empirical knowledge, and more exact modes of thought, made sharper divisions between the sciences inevitable, and once the increasingly complex machinery of State necessitated a more rigorous separation of ranks and occupations, then the inner unity of human nature was severed too, and a disastrous conflict set its harmonious powers at variance.[46]

In times when everything was still closer together and the threads of human destiny, gifts and forces had not yet been so unwound and tugged out of their complex ball, in times when a single human being was more than single and each was everything he could be – history shows clearly that great, active, good human beings were less rare than in ages when everything is separated, each is supposed to serve with only a single force or a single forcelet of his soul, and for the rest groans under a miserable mechanism. I take the Greeks in their fairest time as an example. What might a man then be![47]

Anxiety about the possible effects on the individual worker of the sort of specialized and limited labor now commonplace within the modern economy were not confined to its critics. Adam Smith had acknowledged it as a serious problem:

In the progress of the division of labour, the employment of the far greater part of those who live by labour, that is, of the great body of the people, comes to be confined to a few very simple operations, frequently to one or two. But the understandings of the greater part of men are necessarily formed by their ordinary employments. The man whose whole life is spent in performing a few simple operations . . . has no occasion to exercise his understanding, or to exercise his invention in finding out expedients for removing difficulties which occur. He naturally loses, therefore, the habit of such exertion, and generally becomes as stupid and ignorant as it is possible for a human being to become. The torpor of his mind renders him, not only incapable of relishing or bearing a part in any rational conversation, but of conceiving of any generous, noble, or tender sentiment, and consequently of forming any just judgement concerning many even of the ordinary duties of private life. Of the great and extensive interests of his country, he is altogether incapable of judging; and unless very particular pains have been taken to render him otherwise, he is equally incapable of defending his country in war.[48]

Such a laborer was unfit to perform the proper duties of a citizen – defending his country, deliberating on public affairs, and acting justly in private life – and that had serious implications for the well-being of society. Smith therefore emphasized the need for the state to provide an education that would compensate for this tendency, in order to protect the gains of modernity for society as a whole. For the German playwright, poet, and essayist Friedrich Schiller, however, the "antagonism of powers" within the individual and the race, the one-sided development of different capacities, was at best a means towards human development, not an end in itself; it emphasized the need for a higher stage, in which humanity would return to harmony and nature. A society in which individuals continued to suffer the effects of fragmentation, whatever the gains for the world as a whole, was unacceptable. "In what relation would we stand to past and future ages, if the development of human nature made such a sacrifice necessary? We would have been the serfs of humanity, we would have carried on its slave work for centuries, and impressed on our mutilated nature the shameful traces of this servitude."[49] The alienating effects of the division of labor that characterized modernity must be overcome.[50]

Marx offered a similar perspective, focusing on the consequences of the alienation of the worker from his or her labor both as the necessary condition for the development of capitalism and as its greatest crime against humanity:

> In what does this alienation of labour consist? First, that the work is *external* to the worker, that it is not part of his nature, that consequently he does not fulfil himself in his work but denies himself, has a feeling of misery, not of well-being, does not develop freely a mental and physical energy, but is physically exhausted and mentally debased. The worker therefore feels himself at home only during his leisure, whereas at work he feels homeless. His work is not voluntary but imposed, *forced labour*. It is not the satisfaction of a need, but only a *means* for satisfying other needs.[51]

Marx echoes Schiller in his emphasis on the evils of one-sided development – "at the same time that machine-work exhausts the nervous system to the uttermost, it suppresses the many-sided play of the muscles and confiscates every free bodily and mental action. Even the lightening of the labour becomes a means of torture, since the machine does not free the worker from the work but deprives his work of all meaning"[52] – and in his recourse to the Greeks as the model for what a human being can, and should, be. "We are struck with admiration when we see among the Ancients the same person distinguishing himself to a high degree as philosopher, poet, orator, historian, priest, administrator, general of an army. Our souls are appalled at the sight of such a vast domain."[53] "The individual can never appear here in the dot-like isolation in which he appears as mere free worker."[54] Again, the aim is not to return to Greek society, where the development of the free, well-rounded individual had been at the expense of the enslavement of others, but to recreate its essential qualities at a higher stage.[55]

The Decline of the Organic Community

> That polyp-like nature of the Greek states, in which every human enjoyed an unsubordinated life and could, when there was need, become a whole, now made way for an ingenious clock-work, where, out of the patching-together of countless, but lifeless, parts, a mechanical collective life was formed. Torn apart from one another now were State and Church, laws and customs; enjoyment was divided from labour, the means from the end, the effort from the reward.
>
> F. Schiller, *Über die ästhetische Erziehung des Menschen* 6.7

The contrasts which Schiller and others identified in their analysis of individual development under the conditions of modernity were repeated in their comments on modern society as a whole: natural and unnatural, harmony and discord, wholeness and fragmentation, Greece and today. Greek society had been like coral, at once an indissoluble unity and a composite made up of thousands of individuals. In the course of subsequent developments, however, rather than developing into a higher form of organic being, individual life had been extinguished and social life consisted merely of "a common and clumsy mechanism." This characterization of modern social life as inorganic and artificial became a common cause of complaint against "our modern world, of which the whole civilisation is, to a much greater degree than the civilisation of Greece or Rome, mechanical and external, and tends constantly to become more so."[56]

It was clearly important for critics of modernity to insist that the present condition of the people was "in no way a normal product of real human nature, but rather the artificial outcome of your denaturalised culture."[57] The problem was not society in itself, but rather modern society. All "civilization" could of course be contrasted with the imagined original state of nature, as in Rousseau's analysis; not only in negative terms but also positively, as having brought about a remarkable change in man "by substituting justice for instinct in his conduct, and endowing his actions with the morality they previously lacked."[58] Few writers wished to abandon all the benefits of civilization and society in favor of a wholly natural existence; what mattered was the contrast between those societies where the loss of the "advantages from nature" was balanced by the great advantages to be gained from a sociable life, which "out of a stupid and bounded animal made an intelligent being and a man"[59] – and those societies which reduced humanity to a lower state than before. The danger of modernity, as Schiller thought, was that "egoism has founded its system right in the heart of the most refined sociability, and without any development of a sociable spirit we experience all the infections and all the torments of society."[60]

The most detailed elaboration of this sort of contrast is found in Ferdinand Tönnies' sociological discussion of the distinction between *Gemeinschaft* (community) and *Gesellschaft* (society), "the artificial construction of an aggregate of human beings."[61]

> All praise of rural life has pointed out that the Gemeinschaft among people is stronger there and more alive; it is the lasting and genuine form of living together. In contrast to Gemeinschaft, Gesellschaft is transitory and superficial. Accordingly, Gemeinschaft should be understood as a living organism, Gesellschaft as a mechanical aggregate and artefact.[62]

Tönnies' account characterizes these two forms of sociability through a series of contrasts, all with powerful associations: nature versus artifice, continuity versus change, depth versus superficiality.[63] In the *Gemeinschaft*, individuals are motivated by communal spirit and bound closely together by ties of kinship, religion, shared culture, and multi-layered personal relationships. The *Gesellschaft* is focused on individual self-interest, held together through the necessity of cooperation within a complex division of labor but prone to internal conflict. It is made clear that these two forms of sociability are abstract models ("normal types," in Tönnies' terminology), so that one would always expect to find a mixture of the two tendencies in any historical society; even in modern society *Gesellschaft* is not (yet) entirely dominant, while earlier forms of society always show its tendencies in embryonic form. However, the association of *Gemeinschaft* with the pre-modern past is deliberate and unmistakable, and the example of the Greek *polis*, showing how the desirable qualities of *Gemeinschaft* could be found even in an advanced urban civilization, is central to Tönnies' argument. *Gesellschaft*, meanwhile, is emphatically presented as inferior and inadequate compared with the true organic community, having been imposed on humanity rather than arising spontaneously from its real desires, needs, and nature.

The key to understanding why modern society should be so different from its predecessors was to understand the underlying principles of social development, and at least part of the key to that was historical comparison. As Mill argued, political science was "deduced from the tendencies of things, tendencies known either through our general experience of human nature, or as the result of an analysis of the course of history, considered as a progressive evolution."[64] The pioneering French sociologist Emile Durkheim went further in his emphasis on the latter:

> Social phenomena can only be explained historically; they are all the result of an evolution. Now, what does the idea of evolution imply? That things do not remain identical with themselves, that something new, which did not exist before, comes into being, appears at a given moment; and social evolution is an uninterrupted succession of new phenomena of this kind. Nature, on the contrary, is by definition that which does not change, that which is ever immutable.[65]

Analysis of the course of history overwhelmingly endorsed this view of the transient nature of social arrangements, and also highlighted the limitations of earlier perspectives and prescriptions. As Mill noted, "no two ages, and scarcely any two countries," had come to the same decisions about what rules should be imposed on society, and "yet the people of any given age and country no more suspect any difficulty in it, than if it were a subject on which mankind had always been agreed."[66] However, while there was widespread faith in the capacity of some version of modern social science to establish a full understanding of the character and trajectory of modern society, the results were various, and frequently contradictory. A list of the symptoms or characteristics of modernity in social terms was more or less agreed upon, but their relative importance, let alone their possible causes or the principles on which one might determine this, remained a matter of intense debate.

One approach to the subject was to see social change as one of the products of the overall world-historical process, the underlying dynamic of which shaped every aspect of human life. An obvious example of this is Hegel's philosophical account, in which the course of world history is seen in terms of "the *steps* in the development of the principle whose *content* is the consciousness of freedom."[67] Social institutions and social behavior for Hegel reflect the degree of development of the spirit at any given stage: "no one is left behind by his time, and still less can he skip over it."[68] In his early writings, he had identified the Greek *polis* as a model of political community which might be recreated through the establishment of a new form of *Volksreligion* to bind people together; after 1806, however, he came to regard the instinctive and absolute subordination of the ancient citizen to the collective as a limitation on the development of freedom.[69] Greek institutions embodied an "inadequate individuation," as the principle of personal individuality flourished only within the city community; this is the "adolescence of humanity," while the Roman world, where the process of social differentiation was carried to an extreme, represents the "bitter labour of the manhood of history."[70] Within this grand scheme of development, modern society represents the reconciliation of the struggles and dichotomies that had characterized earlier stages: "The present world has stripped off its barbarism and unjust arbitrariness, and truth has put aside its world of beyond and its casual power. Thus the genuine reconciliation has become objective fact, revealing the State to be the image and the actuality of Reason."[71]

At the other end of the spectrum between idealist and materialist views of society and history stands Marx, who regarded social development as influenced and limited, if not wholly determined, by the development of the productive process.[72] "Assume particular stages of development in production, commerce and consumption, and you will have a corresponding social constitution, a corresponding organisation of the family, of orders or of classes, in a word, a corresponding civil society."[73] "Legal relations as well as forms of the state could neither be understood by themselves, nor explained by the so-called progress of the human mind, but rather have their roots in the material conditions of life."[74] The condition of modern society, therefore, is a direct result of the division of labor, the class conflicts, and the alienation characteristic of capitalism, and therefore stands as a constant reminder of the failures and limitations of capitalism as a way of organizing human life: "At the same pace that mankind masters nature, man seems to become enslaved to other men or to his own infamy . . . All our invention and progress seem to result in endowing material forces with intellectual life, and in stultifying human life into a material force."[75]

Despite their radically different premises, these accounts have a good deal in common; above all, the conception, which Marx took over wholesale from Hegel, of the history of society as a series of discrete stages, each one qualitatively different from the next but in total revealing a coherent principle of development over time. Both interpretations clearly establish modernity as something fundamentally separate from earlier forms of society, defined by a distinctive consciousness and a distinctive form of production respectively. In both cases, the contrast with classical antiquity is essential, as it represents a stage which had to be overcome in order to allow human potential to develop fully and which is nevertheless still regarded with nostalgia (Marx describing it as the "beautiful childhood" in which one takes delight, as Hegel had characterized it as adolescence) and which may, at least in the case of Marx, stand for everything which is lacking from present society and must be re-established at a higher stage.[76]

It was, and is, easy to criticize these approaches as excessively abstract and schematic. Most studies of social history offered more detailed accounts of one or other of the institutions or phenomena that were, for Hegel and Marx, merely reflections or symptoms of the overall world-historical process. They tended to interpret historical development as an ongoing process, with periods of acceleration or deceleration, progress or decline (classical Greece and Rome standing with modernity as chief representatives of the former category, the decline of the Roman Empire and the Middle Ages epitomizing the latter), while retaining, without the sort of explicit theoretical framework that underpinned the Hegelian or Marxian narratives, a conventional sense of history divided into distinct periods. The contrast between antiquity and modernity was therefore not established in such absolute or explicit terms as in the grand narratives of world history, but it remained a constant theme; modern society stood as the culmination of development, the highest degree of intensification – frequently, though not invariably, with a sense that the process had by this point advanced too far. Within the medley of different theories of social development, it is possible to identify three general themes, each one overlapping with and capable of subsuming the others: the development of new institutions in response to new conditions, especially economic; the establishment of limitations on the freedom of action of individuals; and the progressive enthronement of reason as the organizing principle of society.

The first theme has already been touched upon in the discussion of the scale and complexity of modern society. The idea that social forms were changing because they were no longer adequate for modern conditions was expounded most explicitly in discussions of the institutions of representative government and its consequences for the political community; however, this was not the only way in which the development of "industrial society" and the modern economy were seen to promote social change. For Rousseau, as for Smith, the development of private property and the accumulation of wealth necessitated the establishment of law and the institutions of justice, above all civil government – and thereby, in Rousseau's view, instituted inequality as a defining principle of modern social life: "civil government, in so far as it is instituted for the security of property, is in reality instituted for the defence of the rich against the poor."[77] The institution of money could be seen as a simple means of facilitating exchange between relative strangers, but it could equally be presented both as a symptom of the depersonalization of relationships within a complex, heterogeneous society and as one of the agents accelerating this development: "it makes possible relationships between people but leaves them personally undisturbed."[78] "In the past it was possible to regulate ethically the personal relations between master and slave precisely because they were personal relations. But it is not possible to regulate . . . the relations between the shifting holders of mortgages and the shifting debtors of the banks that issue those mortgages; for in this case, no personal bonds of any sort exist" – despite the importance of economic relations in modern life.[79] Above all, economic change was seen to be bound up with a transformation of the values of society, with far-reaching consequences for the nature of sociability; an issue which will be considered in the next section.

The function of institutions such as property law and impersonal exchange could also be understood more generally as setting limits on human freedom of action as a basic requirement for cooperation and social life. This perspective, and the idea that social development should be seen in terms of the progress of "civility" or "civilization" in regulating human behavior, is analyzed at length by Mill. "What makes all the savage communities poor and feeble? The same cause which prevented the lions and tigers from long ago extirpating the race of men – incapacity of co-operation. It is only civilized beings who can combine. All combination is compromise: it is the sacrifice of some portion of individual will, for a common purpose."[80] "All that makes existence valuable to any one, depends on the enforcement of restraints upon the actions of other people. Some rules of conduct, therefore, must be imposed, by law in the first place, and by opinion on many things which are not fit subjects for the operation of law."[81] The same emphasis on the necessity for restraint on individual will as a prerequisite for social life is found later in the theories of Sigmund Freud.

> We believe that civilisation has been created under the pressure of the exigencies of life at the cost of satisfaction of the instincts; and we believe that civilisation is to a large extent being constantly created anew, since each individual who makes a fresh entry into human society repeats this sacrifice of instinctual satisfaction for the benefit of the whole community.[82]

Here, however, there is a different evaluation of the nature and gravity of the sacrifice that might be involved in the social compromise: it consists for Freud in the renunciation not just of a portion of individual will, as Mill suggests, but of "instinctual satisfaction" – that is to say, happiness.

Debates about the appropriate balance between individual liberty and the good of society as a whole, and whether the institutions that formally or informally held the community together, like religion or the state, represented an unacceptable restriction on individual will, dominated the late eighteenth and early nineteenth centuries. The problem was described succinctly by Kant as the "unsocial sociability" of men:

> That is, their tendency to come together in society, coupled, however, with a continual resistance which constantly threatens to break this society up. Man has an inclination to *live in society*, since he feels in this state more like a man, that is, he feels able to develop his natural capacities. But he also has a great tendency to *live as an individual*, to isolate himself.[83]

There was frequent recourse to ancient examples, either to establish universal principles (Aristotle's definition of humanity as *politikon zöon*, a political or social creature, was frequently cited) or to historicize different forms of social organization (one might compare Simmel's argument that only modernity develops a clear and comprehensive concept of the Ego, "as shown by the significance of the problem of liberty which was unknown in ancient times").[84] On the one hand, Rousseau argued that the ancient state had provided the perfect combination of liberty and community, as shown by the fact that it did not need to introduce heavy restraints or punishments for citizens because all were held together by common spirit.[85] On the other hand, Hegel emphasized the necessity of control as the means to real liberty: "Freedom as the ideal form of immediacy and naturalness is not something that is immediate and natural, but on the contrary had to be earned and won, and that through an unceasing process of cultivation of knowledge and will."[86] Far from representing a model of perfection, Greece could be seen to mark the beginning of the conflict that was only now capable of being resolved: "the subject wants to have the consciousness of being substantial in himself as subject, and therefore there arises in this freedom a new conflict between an end for the state and one for himself as an inherently free individual. Such a clash had already begun at the time of Socrates."[87] Meanwhile, Constant contrasted the liberty of the ancients and the moderns and its relation to their influence on the state – "the ancients, although they sacrificed this independence to political rights, sacrificed less to obtain more" – and the German scholar and statesman Wilhelm von Humboldt argued that the correct balance between liberty and discipline could only be established for particular historical conditions; the level of subordination to the community which had been appropriate for Greece was unacceptable now that men had reached a far higher pitch of civilization.[88]

> With respect to those limitations of freedom, however, which do not so much affect the state as the individuals who compose it, we are led to notice a vast difference between ancient and modern governments. The ancients devoted their attention more exclusively to the harmonious development of the individual man, as man; the moderns are chiefly solicitous about his comfort, his prosperity, his productiveness. The former looked to virtue, the latter seek for happiness. And hence it follows that the restrictions imposed on freedom in the ancient states were, in some important respects, more oppressive and dangerous than those which characterise our times.[89]

The Greek state could equally well serve, as in Schiller's analysis, as the exemplar of the harmonious reconciliation of individual and communal interests that must be recaptured at a higher stage of development, or as an example of the unacceptable subordination of the individual to the collective that characterized pre-modern societies. Life in a small, tightly-knit community could be seen as suffocating and claustrophobic; so too could life in the constant sociability of modernity, as the Danish theologian Søren Kierkegaard argued: "In antiquity as well as in the Middle Ages there was an awareness of this longing for solitude and a respect for what it means; whereas in the constant sociability of our day we shrink from solitude to the point that no use for it is known other than as a punishment for criminals."[90] For Rousseau, the loss of communal spirit led not to a liberated but to an impoverished and limited social life: "sociable man, always outside himself, is capable of living only in the opinion of others and, so to speak, derives the sentiment of his own existence solely from their judgement."[91]

> Before Art had fashioned our manners and taught our passions to speak in ready-made terms, our morals were rustic but natural; and differences in conduct conveyed differences of character at first glance. Human nature was, at bottom, no better; but men found their security in how easily they saw through one another . . . One no longer dares to appear what one is; and under this perpetual constraint, the men who make up the herd that is called society will, when placed in similar circumstances, all act in similar ways unless more powerful motives induce them differently. One will thus never know with whom one is dealing . . . No more sincere friendships, no more real esteem; no more well-founded trust. Suspicions, offences, fears, coolness, reserve, hatred, betrayal, will constantly hide between this even and deceitful veil of politeness.[92]

The modern development of more elaborate institutions and forms of sociability, and above all the creation of a sophisticated state apparatus and legal system, could be seen as the fulfillment of the Enlightenment vision of a society organized according to reason; the underlying principle of modernity was frequently identified as "rationalization." Mill's defense of modern society rests not only on the existence of a high degree of cooperation but also on the fact that its laws are based on rational principles rather than tradition and superstition; the reason why previous eras were unable to agree on the best social order is precisely that they relied on custom rather than reason.[93] Humboldt contrasted ancient and modern political thought in a similar manner: "We ought not to forget, moreover, in our admiration of antiquity, that what we are so apt to consider the results of wisdom in the ancient legislators was mostly nothing more than the effect of popular custom."[94] The economist Alfred Marshall noted the fact that earlier political economists had often praised capitalism when it was most destructive of traditional social and economic structures: "This was partly because they saw clearly what we of this generation have in a great measure forgotten, the cruelty of the yoke of custom and rigid ordinance which it had displaced."[95] In contrast to the usual condemnations of modern values, "it is deliberateness, and not selfishness, that is the characteristic of the modern age."[96] Finally, Durkheim observed the effects of the process on the established order:

> Our faith has been troubled, tradition has lost its sway; individual judgement has been freed from collective judgement . . . The remedy for the evil is not to seek to resuscitate traditions and practices which, no longer responding to present conditions of society, can only live an artificial, false existence.[97]

The undermining of tradition was disturbing for the individual, but offered grounds for optimism. Durkheim argued strongly that modern society, because it was a human creation, was always open to reform, in contrast to a society legitimated by (purportedly) unchanging and inviolable tradition: "The rules which constitute it [modern society] do not have a constraining force which snuffs out free thought; but, because they are rather made for us and, in a certain sense, by us, we are free. We wish to understand them; we do not fear to change them."[98]

In Weber and Tönnies, however, we find a more skeptical account of the implications of rationalization, which focused less on Greece – the archetype of the pre-modern "natural" (and hence not rationalized) community – than on Rome, the first great example of the process now brought to its highest level of development in modernity. For Weber, the key analytical concept is "bureaucracy," the most rational form of social organization, that which is capable of the highest levels of technical efficiency and is most closely associated with the development of modern society – above all the state apparatus, but increasingly every form of modern social grouping.[99] The increasing dominance of bureaucracy in modern society accentuates the alienation of the mass of the population from the state – "modern parliaments are primarily representative bodies of those ruled by bureaucratic means" – and subordinates all ethical or political considerations to means–end rationality.[100] It replaces the arbitrary but human rule of the lord, operating by personal sympathy and favor, with the rule of the detached and objective expert.[101] It undermines the basis of community, and threatens the "vigor" of society: "it may be said that 'normally' – though not without exception – the vigour to expand is directly related to the degree of bureaucratization," with Rome and Britain offered as examples of empires in which the degree of bureaucratization was relatively limited.[102] The problem for modern society was that, as a result of the process of rationalization, "traditional authority," the primary form of legitimation of authority in earlier societies, was now scarcely tenable; reaction against the excesses of bureaucracy was therefore likely to lead to a rejection of all legal, rational authority and a recourse to the potent but unpredictable force of charisma:

> The bureaucratic order merely replaces the belief in the sanctity of traditional norms by compliance with rationally determined rules and by the knowledge that these rules can be superseded by others, if one has the necessary power, and hence are not sacred. But charisma, in its most potent forms, disrupts rational rule as well as tradition altogether and overturns all notions of sanctity . . . In this purely empirical and value-free sense charisma is indeed the specifically creative revolutionary force of history.[103]

Tönnies developed an even more explicit warning of the possible consequences of modern social developments, emphasizing the connection between the development of rational law in the Later Roman Empire and its social disintegration:

> In the beginning it seems quite innocent, it means nothing but progress, refinement, improvement, and facilitations; it stands for fairness, reason and enlightenment. This form persisted even in the moral decay of the Empire. Both trends, the elaboration, universalizing and finally systematizing and codification of the law, on the one hand, and, on the other hand, the decay of life and *mores* along with brilliant political successes, capable administration and an efficient and liberal jurisprudence, have often been described. But only a few seem to have realised the necessary connection between, and the unity and interdependence of, these trends. Even the learned writers are seldom able to free themselves from prejudices and to arrive at an unbiased , strictly objective view of the physiology and pathology of social life. They admire the Roman Empire and the Roman law; they abhor the decay of the family and of *mores*. But they are unable to discuss the causal relationship between the two phenomena.[104]

The two faces of rationalization are clearly inseparable, just as liberation from the restrictions of custom and tradition was inseparable from the destruction of the basis for communal solidarity:

> A rational, scientific and independent law was made possible only through the emancipation of the individuals from all the ties which bound them to the family, the land and the city, and which held them to superstition, faith, traditions, habit and duty. Such liberation meant the fall of the communal household in village and town, of the agricultural community, and of the art of the town as a fellowship, religious, patriotic craft. It meant the victory of egoism, impudence, falsehood and cunning, the ascendancy of greed for money, ambition and lust for pleasure. But it also brought the victory of the contemplative, clear and sober consciousness in which scholars and cultured men now dare to approach things human and divine. And this process can never be considered completed.[105]
>
> It extinguishes differences and inequalities, gives all the same behavior, the same way of speech and expression, the same money, the same culture, the same cupidity, and the same curiosity. It forms the abstract human being, the most artificial, regular, and unscrupulous type of machinery, which appears as a ghost in broad daylight.[106]

Values and Vigorousness

Whether it was regarded as the cause or the consequence of the destruction of traditional structures, the rationalization of society, or the one-sided development of the individual, there was widespread agreement – with Hegel standing as almost the sole exception – that the "spirit" of modern society, and the values that modernity embodied, constituted strong grounds for regarding it as inferior to earlier forms, or, at best, as having not yet realized its potential. Modernity was criticized for pursuing wrong values, for taking certain values to excess, or for lacking the right values – or, as Comte argued, for lacking values altogether:

> Manifestly, society, regarded from a moral point of view, is in a condition of real and profound Anarchy . . . This anarchy results, in the last resort, from the absence of any preponderating system, capable of uniting all minds in a communion of ideas. Minds, no longer united by any real bond, diverge on all essential points, with that licence which unregulated individualism

must produce. Hence the entire absence of public morality; the universal spread of egotism; the preponderance of considerations purely material; and, as a last inevitable consequence, corruption erected into a system of government, as being the only kind of order applicable to a population become deaf to all appeals made in the name of a general ideal and alive only to the voice of private interest.[107]

More commonly, critics focused on modernity's lack of particular values or qualities that were identified as socially or personally desirable, above all on the basis of their role in earlier societies: piety, civic spirit, loyalty, heroism. John Stuart Mill acknowledged the progress which the moderns had made in moral philosophy and the conception of the ideal standard of human character,

> not the moral conceptions of heroes or philosophers which measure the difference between one age and another, so much as the accepted popular standard of virtuous conduct.
>
> Taking that as the criterion, and comparing the best Grecian with the best modern community, is the superiority wholly on the side of the moderns? Has there not been deterioration as well as improvement, and the former perhaps as marked as the latter? . . . We greatly doubt if most of the positive virtues were not better conceived, and more highly prized, by the public opinion of Greece than by that of Great Britain; while negative and passive qualities have now engrossed the chief part of the honour paid to virtue; and it may be questioned if even private duties are, on the whole, better understood, while duties to the public, unless in cases of special trust, have almost dropped out of the catalogue: that idea, so powerful in the free states of Greece, has faded into a mere rhetorical ornament.[108]

Modern virtue was seen to be largely passive – the avoidance of doing wrong, rather than an active drive to do right – and inward-looking, centered on private rather than public affairs. It was difficult to distinguish such behavior, rational though it might be, from outright selfishness. Tönnies emphasized the problems of a society dominated by individualism rather than by a common spirit:

> Everybody here is by himself and isolated, and there exists a condition of tension against all others . . . Such a negative attitude towards one another becomes the normal and always underlying relation of those power-endowed individuals, and it characterises the Gesellschaft in the condition of rest: no one wants to grant and produce anything for another individual, nor will

he be inclined to give ungrudgingly to another individual, unless in exchange for a gift or labour equivalent that he considers at least equal to what he has given.[109]

The absence of a sense of public duty and communal spirit could equally be presented as an excess of individualism, a virtue taken to extremes. Paradoxically, however, modernity might also be criticized for undervaluing the individual, or at least certain types of individual. In Friedrich Nietzsche's intentionally provocative view, modern society is built around the "herd man" and an unnatural process of "leveling" of individual qualities and abilities, under the banner of "equal rights," that leaves no space for the sort of heroic individual that had characterized Greece:

> The herd man in Europe today gives himself the appearance of being the only permissible kind of man and glorifies his attributes, which make him tame, easy to get along with, and useful to the herd, as if they were the truly human virtues: namely, public spirit, benevolence, industriousness, moderation, modesty, indulgence and pity.[110]

This is of a piece with Nietzsche's critique of modern morality as "slavish" and his espousal of aristocratic values in forthright opposition to democracy and socialism.[111]

> The great men of antique morality, Epictetus for instance, knew nothing of the now normal glorification of thinking for others, of living for others; in the light of our moral fashion they would have to be called downright immoral, for they strove with all their might *for* their *ego* and *against* feeling with others . . . Perhaps they would reply to us: "If you are so boring or ugly an object to yourself, by all means think of others more than of yourself!"[112]

However, Nietzsche was not the only writer to evoke a contrast between ancient and modern on this issue:

> The dialectic of antiquity was orientated to the eminent (the great individual – and then the crowd; one free individual, and then the slaves); at present the dialectic of Christianity is orientated to representation (the majority perceive themselves in the representative and are liberated by the awareness that he is representing them in a kind of self-consciousness) . . . Whereas in antiquity the host of individuals existed, so to speak, in order

to determine how much the excellent individual was worth, today the coinage standard has been changed so that about so and so many human beings uniformly make one individual; thus it is only a matter of getting the proper number – and then one has significance. In antiquity the individual in the crowd had no significance whatsoever; the man of excellence stood for them all.[113]

Part of the problem, according to Nietzsche's analysis, was that qualities which could in the right context, for a particular individual, be heroic – the asceticism of the classical philosopher, for example – had been taken to excess, so that they became destructive, and elevated as the guiding principle of the whole of society, with devastating consequences for those individuals who had the capacity for greater, or different, things.[114] The idea that modernity's problem was one of excess was found in a wide range of writers of quite different political sympathies, focusing above all on the excessive development of "civilization" in modern society. As Kant, for example, put it, "we are *civilised* to the point of excess in all kinds of social courtesies and proprieties."[115] "It was quite otherwise with the ancient Greeks," argued Schiller. "With them civilisation did not manifest itself to such an extent that nature was abandoned in consequence."[116] Rousseau held up the Spartans and the Romans as a standing reproach to those who favored refinement over heroism and virtue – "it is more comfortable to live where things are so constituted that everyone is exempt from being a good man" – while Mill devoted an essay to considering the drawbacks as well as the advantages of modernity's advances: "one of the effects of a high state of civilization upon character, is a relaxation of individual energy: or rather, the concentration of it within the narrow sphere of the individual's money-getting pursuits."[117] Power over nature had brought freedom from much of the suffering endured by earlier generations, but at a price:

It is in avoiding the presence not only of actual pain, but of whatever suggests offensive or disagreeable ideas, that a great part of refinement consists. We may remark too, that this is possible only by a perfection of mechanical arrangements impractical in any but a high state of civilization . . . The consequence is that, compared with former times, there is in the more opulent classes of modern civilized communities much more of the amiable and humane, and much less of the heroic . . . There has crept over the refined classes, over the whole class of gentlemen in England, a moral effeminacy, an inaptitude for every kind of struggle.[118]

"Are the decay of individual energy, the weakening of the influence of superior minds over the multitude, the growth of charlatanerie, and the diminished efficacy of public opinion as a restraining power, – are these the price we necessarily pay for the benefits of civilization?"[119] "This torpidity and cowardice . . . is new in the world: but modified by the different temperaments of different nations, it is a natural consequence of the progress of civilization."[120] This is not too far from Nietzsche's denunciation of "the effeminate idea of modern humanity."[121] Durkheim also noted the effects: "a great many stimuli formerly agreeable to us have become too strong for us, and, consequently, painful. If we are open to more pleasures, we are also open to more pain."[122]

> Civilization, far from setting us free, in fact creates some new need with every new power it develops in us. The fetters of the physical tighten ever more alarmingly, so that fear of losing what we have stifles even the most burning impulse towards improvement, and the maxim of passive obedience passes for the supreme wisdom of life. Thus do we see the spirit of the age wavering between perversity and brutality, between unnaturalness and mere nature, between superstition and moral unbelief; and it is only through an equilibrium of evils that it is still sometimes kept within bounds.[123]

For Schiller, the problem of modern society was not so much that humanity was rendered less heroic by being freed from concern about physical needs, but rather that those needs had been multiplied enormously and established as the sole aim of existence. In so far as modernity was seen to have values of its own, rather than simply a strange mixture of excess and deficiency in more universal values, they were located above all in its materialism, the pursuit of profit and a narrow understanding of utility. "The ancient politicians forever spoke of morals and of virtue," declared Rousseau. "Ours speak only of commerce and money . . . They appraise men like herds of cattle."[124] Marx drew on Aristotle to draw a clear contrast between the idea of limited economic activity for a specific end that had characterized antiquity and capitalism's eternal pursuit of gain as an end in itself; the former subordinated exchange to human and communal needs, the latter established it as the ruling principle of society.[125] For others, too, the strongest indictment of modernity was that the ends for which individual development was stifled and freedom restricted were so limited, unworthy, and inadequate:

If he bargains away the product of his toil, all that remains to him is its mere money-worth; and thus his energy can never rise above the character of the busy strokes of a machine; in his eyes it is but weariness and bitter, sorrowful toil. The latter is the lot of the slave of industry; and our modern factories offer us the sad picture of the deepest degradation of man – constant labour, killing both body and soul, without joy or love, almost without aim.[126]

Are you accomplices in the current folly of the nations – the folly of wanting above all to produce as much as possible and to become as rich as possible? What you ought to do, rather, is to hold up to them the counter-reckoning: how great a sum of *inner* value is thrown away in pursuit of this external goal? But where is your inner value if you no longer know what it is to breathe freely? If you no longer possess the slightest power over yourselves? If you all too often grow weary of yourselves like a drink that has been left too long standing?[127]

The counterpoint to such materialism and externalization was of course ancient Greece, a society founded on the development of mind, spirit, and body, interior and exterior, in harmony. However, whereas Marx condemned the way that labor, the basic activity of human existence, had become alienated and alienating because of the particular spirit of capitalism, Nietzsche's complaint against modernity was that labor, the basic activity of the herd but not of the heroic spirit, had been elevated into the highest principle of life.[128] Each claimed support from classical philosophy for their views.

It could scarcely be claimed that acquisitiveness was unique to modernity. It could be, and frequently was, argued that it had now become the central principle of human existence, but it was also suggested that modern acquisitiveness was somehow different, and that this explained its dominance over modern society. Marx argued that the difference lay in the ultimate ends of the activity; for Weber, what was distinctly modern was not the acquisitive drive itself but the application of rational methods in its service.[129] Economic theory took such rationality for granted; Weber emphasized that it was a historically limited phenomenon, whose emergence needed to be understood, above all because of the obvious impediments to its development.

Every such attempt at explanation must, recognising the fundamental importance of the economic factor, above all take account of the economic conditions. But at the same time the opposite correlation must not be left out of consideration. For though the development of economic rationalism is partly dependent on rational techniques and law, it is at the same time determined by the ability and disposition of men to adopt certain types of practical rational conduct. When these types have been obstructed by spiritual obstacles, the development of rational economic conduct has also met serious inner resistance. The magical and religious forces, and the ethical ideas of duty based upon them, have in the past always been among the most important formative influences on conduct.[130]

"Devotion to the cause of making money" is now intimately bound up with the capitalist system, to the point where "it no longer needs the support of any religious forces, and feels the attempts of religion to influence economic life, in so far as they can still be felt at all, to be as much an unjustified interference as its regulation by the state."[131] In earlier forms of society, however, men were driven by quite different motives, to which the acquisitive manner of life was quite alien.

It is just that which seems to the pre-capitalist man so incomprehensible and mysterious, so unworthy and contemptible. That anyone should be able to make it the sole purpose of his life-work, to sink into the grave weighed down with a great material load of money and goods, seems to him explicable only as the product of a perverse instinct, the *auri sacra fames.*[132]

Modern mentality is quite alien to that of earlier periods, but it cannot have emerged from nowhere; its roots must be found in the ways of thinking appropriate to pre-capitalist society, and, echoing Nietzsche, Weber finds them in the Christian principles of asceticism and renunciation.[133] What truly defines the spirit of modernity, however, and separates it utterly from the pre-modern world, is that this renunciation – "a departure from an age of full and beautiful humanity, which can no more be repeated in the course of our cultural development than can the flower of the Athenian culture of antiquity" – is no longer a matter of choice:

The Puritan wanted to work in a calling; we are forced to do so. For when asceticism was carried out of monastic cells into everyday life, and began to dominate worldly morality, it did its part in building the tremendous cosmos the modern economic order. This order is now bound to the technical and economic conditions of machine production which today determine the lives of all the individuals who are born into this mechanism, not only those directly concerned with economic acquisition, with irresistible force. Perhaps it will so determine them until the last ton of fossilized coal is burnt. In Baxter's view the case for external goods should only lie on the shoulders of the 'saint like a light cloak, which can be thrown aside at any moment.' But fate decreed that the cloak should become an iron cage.

Since asceticism undertook to remodel the world and to work out its ideals in the world, material goods have gained an increasing and finally an inexorable power over the lives of men as at no previous period in history. Today the spirit of religious asceticism – whether finally, who knows? – has escaped from the cage. But victorious capitalism, since it rests on mechanical foundations, needs its support no longer. The rosy blush of its laughing heir, the Enlightenment, seems also to be irresistibly fading, and the idea of duty in one's calling prowls about in our loves like the ghost of dead religious beliefs.[134]

Return to the Greeks?

Let us give up the desire and hope of making our fellow citizens into a people of Greeks and Romans. We can do much better than that. Our modern customs, our northerly location, the great size of our states almost equal in civilization, together with the relations between them, the invention of paper and printing, our progress in the sciences, navigation, commerce and the postal service, all make it our law to avoid servile copying of the ancients, to be ourselves, to attain the only degree of improvement and happiness of which we are capable.

J.-B. Say, article for the *Décade Philosophique*, 21–2

Throughout the nineteenth century, a succession of commentators came to the conclusion that the level of happiness attainable under the conditions of modern society was significantly inferior to that enjoyed by the Greeks and Romans; the only hope that this might change in the future was through the sort of "total revolution" in the structures of society advocated by writers like Schiller or Marx. The comparison of antiquity and modernity established what was distinctive about modern society, and revealed the underlying principles of historical development that had brought it into being; it also emphasized what had been lost in the transition. As Bernard Yack has argued, the identification of new objects of hatred was as important as the development of new ideals in the late eighteenth- and nineteenth-century discourse on society; in the confrontation of ancient and modern, these two developments were indissolubly bound together.[135]

A crucial point of debate was then how far antiquity might offer a useful model for the future of society. The argument was especially fierce around the issues of democracy and the state, perhaps because political structures were most obviously susceptible to reform or abolition in the light of principles derived from the classics.[136] It was always possible to reject ancient ideas and examples as irrelevant to modern conditions – "For the final principle of the constitution, that is to say for the principle of our time, there is nothing that can be learnt from them. With science and art it is quite different."[137] – but it was, and remains, equally possible to read Thucydides or Aristotle as offering an insight into universal principles and political situations. In the development of prescriptions for society, however, classical models were much less prominent. The more that social change was understood as the product of long-term developments and impersonal structures rather than of individual human action, the less likely it appeared that it would be possible to recreate an earlier form of society. "The natural progress of civilisation, therefore, determines with entire certainty for each epoch the improvements of which the social state is susceptible."[138]

> Could we convert a city into a kind of fortified camp, and infuse into each breast so martial a genius, and such a passion for public good, as to make every one willing to undergo the greatest hardships for the sake of the public; these affections might now, as in ancient times, prove alone a sufficient spur to industry, and support the community . . . But as these principles are too disinterested and too difficult to support, it is a requisite to govern men by other passions, and animate them with a spirit of avarice and industry, art and luxury.[139]

> The change which is thus in progress, and to a great extent consummated, is the greatest ever recorded in social affairs: the most complete, the most fruitful in consequences, and the most irrevocable. Whoever can meditate on it, and not see that so great a revolution vitiates all existing rules of government and policy, and renders all practice and all predictions grounded only on prior experience worthless, is wanting in the very first and most elementary principles of statesmanship in these times.[140]

> To seek to realise a civilisation superior to that demanded by the nature of surrounding conditions is to desire to turn illness loose in the very society of which we are part . . . In every epoch there is a certain refinement of civilisation whose sickly character is attested by the uneasiness and restlessness which accompanies it. But there is never anything desirable about sickness.[141]

Social science came to pride itself on its empirical basis, on studying things as they are in contrast to the ancient philosophers' utopian speculation: "What they strove to discover was not the nature and origin of social phenomena, not what they actually are, but what they ought to be."[142] However, this anti-utopianism was clearly not the only basis for the rejection of classical models. Modernity was understood as a unified phenomenon, as a system, whether determined by the principle of rationalization or alienation or the division of labor. The contrast with antiquity, whether in its values, institutions, or spirit, established it as a distinct and unprecedented form of society; it also emphasized that to recreate the society of the Greek *polis* would require the transformation of every aspect of life, and the reversal of apparently irreversible processes. The more that modernity was condemned because of its incompatibility with the Greek ideal, the more that ideal was seen to be irretrievably lost in the past.

Many different, and not necessarily compatible, interpretations of the nature of modernity were expounded, to the point where it could be characterized, by Marx among others, precisely in terms of confusion, fragmentation, constant metamorphosis, and paradox.[143] It is less commonly noted that the same might be said of the image of ancient society that was developed in parallel. The different theories of modernity's essence reflected, at least in part, different ideas of antiquity. None was wholly implausible, but they derived from different nations (Athens, Sparta, or Rome), different periods (the heroic, aristocratic individualism of the Homeric era, the communal values and unity of the Athenian *polis*, or the rationalized, bureaucratic society of the later Empire) and frequently different genres of literature (philosophy, history, tragedy). Antiquity could stand for harmony and heroic individualism, for solidarity and solitude, for civilization and naturalness. The contrasts between Rome and Greece were widely acknowledged, with Rome often presented in terms of proto-modernity; "ancient Greece," however, was all too often treated as a single, distinct, and unified historical period, when it was not simply taken to be emblematic of "classical antiquity" as a whole. The idealization of Greece was never straightforward. In social terms, it could be presented as the polar opposite of modernity and the epitome of the premodern *Gemeinschaft*; as the example of the correct degree of civilization and development, promoting human development while remaining in touch with nature, in contrast to overdeveloped, unnatural, and artificial modernity; or as a more developed, more sophisticated society, which had followed an alternative path. For the purposes of the critique of modernity, what mattered was that one of these versions could be believed to be true and associated with – indeed, offered as the explanation for – the undeniable cultural achievements of antiquity.

Different writers were perfectly able to identify the idealizations and omissions in the historical accounts of their opponents, while naturally maintaining that their own versions were firmly founded in the ancient evidence. A partial exception can be found in Nietzsche's explicit skepticism about the idealization of the Greeks, identifying the psychological roots of the impulse, revealing the uncertain foundations of historical knowledge, and deliberately presenting an internally incoherent account.[144] He then, of course, proceeded to proffer an alternative myth, in order to contrast modernity with a world of reckless, heroic individuals rather than one of harmonious communities:

> I saw all their institutions develop out of precautionary rules in order to make themselves secure against the *explosives* inside them. The immense internal tension discharged itself in terrible and reckless hostility against others; the city communities tore one another to pieces so that each individual citizen could find peace in himself. One simply had to be strong; danger was nearby – it lay in wait everywhere. The magnificent supple physique, the bold realism and immoralism which is peculiar to the Hellene was a necessity, not a "natural quality." It was a consequence, it was not there from the beginning.[145]

Nietzsche was no more immune than others to the attractions of the idea of antiquity as an alternative to modernity, for all his explicit doubts as to whether this idea ever actually existed; for him, as for many others, it offered some hope that the discontents of modernity were not inescapable. Hegel had argued that discontent was simply the most characteristic symptom of modernity – aroused not least through the comparison with an imaginary, idealized past, less developed and yet far superior.

> Vexation is the sentiment of the modern world: the feeling of vexation presupposes an end, a demand of the will, which authorizes and justifies this feeling when the end is not fulfilled. Thus modern man easily develops a mood in which he loses heart for everything else, and does not even seek to reach ends which he could reach . . . This is the feeling of vexation; it could not have formed the character of the Greeks.[146]

Durkheim sought to argue that "at all times man has been disquieted and malcontent. He has always felt that he is pulled apart, divided against himself"; in other words, this might be a symptom of social life in general, but there was no remedy to be found in past societies.[147] For writers like Schiller and Marx, however, the promise of antiquity was not that it could be recreated but that it established the possibility of alternatives to modernity. Marx's account of what "communism" might be like as the successor to capitalism is exceptionally vague; commentators have often tried to establish a clearer vision on the basis of his praise of ancient Greece and criticisms of modern alienation – communism must be the realization of one and antithesis of the other.[148] What mattered most, however, was simply that modernity had not always existed. Through consideration of the past one could then identify the processes or principles that would, or might, lead beyond it, without needing to go into details as to what that higher stage might be. "A man cannot become a child again, or he becomes childish."[149]

> In bourgeois economics – and in the epoch of production to which it corresponds – this complete working-out of the human content appears as a complete emptying-out, this universal objectification as total alienation, and this tearing-down of all limited, one-sided aims as sacrifice of the human end-in-itself to an entirely external end. This is why the childish world of antiquity appears on one side as loftier. On the other side, it really is loftier in all matters where closed shapes, forms and given limits are sought for. It is satisfaction from a limited standpoint, while the modern gives no satisfaction; or, where it appears satisfied with itself, it is *vulgar*.[150]

Notes

1   *Nouveaux principes de l'économie politique*, II, 434.
2   "Plan of the scientific operations necessary for reorganizing society," 142.
3   "Of the industrial system," 153.
4   Gay (1970), 448–96; Outram (1995), 96–113.
5   Say, "Lecture at the Collège de France," 152.
6   Comte, "Plan of the scientific operations," 141.
7   Ibid., 221.
8   "Of the industrial system," 153.
9   Comte, "Plan of the scientific operations," 141.
10   "Civilization," 125.
11   "Grote's History of Greece I," 273.
12   "Grote's History of Greece II," 313.

13 *Discourse on the Origin and Foundations of Inequality*, II.57.
14 *Of the Social Contract*, III.364–5; Yack (1992), 58–9.
15 Yack (1992) xii.
16 Love (1986) 90–4.
17 Schiller, *Über der ästhetische Erziehung*, 6.1–2.
18 Bury, *History of Greece*, I, 68.
19 Cf. Humphreys (1978), 193–208; Loraux (1996).
20 Marx and Engels, *Manifest der Kommunistischen Partei*, 462.
21 On "class" in ancient history, see Morley (2004a), 80–6.
22 Marx and Engels, *Manifest der Kommunistischen Partei*, 463.
23 Weber, *Economy and Society*, 302–7; Finley (1985), 35–61.
24 Wood (1995), 76–107.
25 "German Constitution," 21.
26 Hegel, *Vorlesungen über die Philosophie der Geschichte*, 67.
27 Wokler (2001) 425–36.
28 *Of the Social Contract*, III.12.1–3; cf. III.15.6–7. Yack (1992) 73–81.
29 *Wealth of Nations*, IV.vii.c.77.
30 Constant, "De la liberté," 496, 501; Dodge (1980) 18–51.
31 Hegel, *Aesthetics*, 510.
32 Hegel, "German constitution," 19–20.
33 Constant, "De la liberté," 497.
34 Durkheim, *Division of Labour*, 257–62.
35 Smith, *Wealth of Nations*, V.i.f.51.
36 Ibid., V.i.a.
37 "Civilization," 122.
38 Ibid.
39 Ibid., 124.
40 Comte, *Positive Philosophy*, II, 118; Durkheim, *Division of Labour*, 68, 406–7. McCarthy (2003), 139–41.
41 Durkheim, *Division of Labour*, 41.
42 Ibid., 241.
43 Ibid., 242.
44 *The Protestant Ethic and the Spirit of Capitalism*, 182.
45 On this last point, Yack (1992), 158–9.
46 Schiller, *Über der ästhetische Erziehung*, 6.4–6.
47 Herder, *On the Cognition and Sensation*, 226. See also Schlegel, *Lectures*, I, 215: "The Grecian idea of humanity consisted in a perfect concord and proportion between all the powers – a natural harmony. The moderns again have arrived at the consciousness of the internal discord which renders such an idea impossible."
48 *Wealth of Nations*, V.i.f.50.
49 *Über die ästhetische Erziehung*, 6.14.

50 Kain (1982), 13–33.
51 *Economic and Philosophical Manuscripts of 1844*, 274.
52 *Kapital*, I, 445–6.
53 *Poverty of Philosophy* 11.
54 *Grundrisse* 435.
55 Yack (1992), 181.
56 Arnold, *Culture and Anarchy*, 49.
57 Wagner, *Art-Work of the Future*, 208.
58 *Of the Social Contract*, I.8.1.
59 Ibid.
60 *Über die ästhetische Erziehung*, 5.5.
61 *Community and Society*, 64.
62 Ibid., 35.
63 See generally Mitzman (1973).
64 "Inaugural address to the University of St Andrew's" [1867], quoted in Collini, Winch, and Burrow (1983), 127.
65 Durkheim, review in *L'Année Sociologique*, 61–2.
66 "On liberty," 220.
67 *Vorlesungen über die Philosophie der Geschichte*, 77.
68 Ibid., 72.
69 Yack (1992), 185–223.
70 *Elements of the Philosophy of Right*, §§ 356–7; *Vorlesungen über die Philosophie der Geschichte*, 138.
71 *Elements of the Philosophy of Right*, § 360.
72 On different interpretations of Marx's theory of history see Cohen (1978); Wood (1995) 108–78.
73 Letter from Marx to P. V. Annenkov, December 28, 1846, 96.
74 Marx, *Contribution to the Critique of Political Economy*, 263.
75 Marx, Speech at the Anniversary of the *People's Paper*.
76 Marx, *Grundrisse*, 111.
77 Smith, *Wealth of Nations*, V.i.b; Rousseau, *Discourse on the Origin and Foundations of Inequality*, II.24.
78 Simmel, *Philosophy of Money*, 303; generally, 170–2, 295–303.
79 Weber, "Religious rejections of the world," 331.
80 Mill, "Civilization," 122.
81 Mill, "On liberty," 220.
82 *Introductory Lectures on Psychoanalysis*, 47.
83 "Idea for a universal history," 44.
84 Simmel, *Philosophy of Money*, 64.
85 *Discourse on Political Economy*, 33.
86 *Vorlesungen über die Philosophie der Geschichte*, 58–9.
87 Hegel, *Aesthetics*, 510; Roberts (1994), 214–20.

88　Constant, "De la liberté," 502; Humboldt, *Sphere and Duties of Government*, 65.
89　Humboldt, *Sphere and Duties of Government*, 7.
90　*Sickness Unto Death*, 64.
91　*Discourse on the Origin and Foundations of Inequality*, II.57.
92　Rousseau, *Discourse on the Sciences and Arts*, 12–14.
93　"On liberty," 220.
94　*Sphere and Duties of Government*, 65.
95　*Principles of Economics*, 11–12.
96　Ibid., 6.
97　*Division of Labour*, 145.
98　Ibid., 407–8.
99　"Politics as a vocation," 82.
100　Scaff (1989), 166–70.
101　Weber, *Economy and Society*, 971–94.
102　Ibid., 209–10.
103　Ibid., 1117.
104　*Community and Society*, 202.
105　Ibid.
106　Ibid.
107　"Philosophical considerations on science and the savants," 199.
108　"Grote's History of Greece II," 314.
109　*Community and Society*, 65.
110　*Beyond Good and Evil*, no. 199.
111　Cf. Love (1986), 141–68; Strong (2000).
112　Nietzsche, *Daybreak*, no. 131.
113　Kierkegaard, *Two Ages*, 84–5.
114　Nehemas (1985), 114–18.
115　"Idea for a universal history," 49.
116　"On naïve and sentimental poetry," 190.
117　Rousseau, "Last reply," 76, 78; Roberts (1994), 165–7; Mill, "Civilization," 129.
118　Mill, "Civilization," 131.
119　Ibid., 135.
120　Ibid., 132.
121　Nietzsche, "Homer's Wettkampf," 783.
122　*Division of Labour*, 242.
123　Schiller, *Über die ästhetische Erziehung*, 5.5.
124　Rousseau, *Discourse on the Sciences and Arts*, 41.
125　*Kapital*, I, 73–4, 167 n.6; McCarthy (1994), 33–65.
126　Wagner, *Art and Revolution*, 49.
127　Nietzsche, *Daybreak*, no. 206.

128 Love (1986), 169–94.
129 *Protestant Ethic*, 17–19.
130 Ibid., 26–7.
131 Ibid., 72.
132 Ibid, 71–2.
133 Hennis (1988), 146–62; Scaff (1989), 87–92; McCarthy (2003), 88–92.
134 Weber, *Protestant Ethic*, 181–2.
135 Yack (1992), 6.
136 Roberts (1994); Nelson (2004).
137 Hegel, *Vorlesungen über die Philosophie der Geschichte*, 66.
138 Comte, "Plan of the scientific operations," 147.
139 Hume, "Of commerce," 294–5.
140 Mill, "Civilization," 126.
141 Durkheim, *Division of Labour*, 340–1.
142 Durkheim, "Montesquieu and Rousseau," 57–8.
143 Berman (1982), 89–114.
144 Porter (2000a), 167–288.
145 *Götzen-Dämmerung*, 157.
146 *Lectures on the Philosophy of Religion*, 2.263.
147 "Dualism of human nature," 155.
148 Cf. McCarthy (1990), 104–19; (1994), 67–123.
149 Marx, *Grundrisse*, 111.
150 Ibid., 488.

4

An Aesthetic Education

The Failings of Modern Culture

Beauty appropriate to the age. If our sculptors, painters and composers want
to hit off the spirit of the age they must depict beauty as bloated, gigantic
and nervous, just as the Greeks, under the spell of their morality of modera-
tion, saw and depicted beauty as the Apollo Belvedere. *We* ought really to
call him ugly! But our stupid "classicists" have robbed us of all honesty!
F. Nietzsche, *Daybreak*, no. 161

In social or economic terms, the progress of "civilization" could be presented as a single line of progressive development on which the position
of different societies could be plotted. Modernity might then be seen as
the culmination and goal of this process, or as the highest point yet reached
in the course of history; alternatively it could be seen as having exceeded
the proper or natural limits of development and so begun to undermine
its masculinity and vigor through an excess of refinement. In either
case, there was little dispute that it had advanced well beyond any of its
predecessors. Thinking about the rise of modernity in terms of "culture,"
however, offered a different perspective. The term could be used, as it
was through most of the eighteenth century, simply as a synonym for
"civilization" in the broad sense, but it could also refer to a more specific
aspect of human life – the realms of art, literature, ideas, science, and
spiritual beliefs, as opposed to economics or politics. In this latter sense,
there were serious doubts as to whether modernity had advanced at all
beyond the achievements of its predecessors. Considered in the light
of the artistic achievements of the past and the universal standards that
they were considered to embody, modern art and literature were widely
regarded as disappointing and inadequate.

There was little support for the notion that the standards of the past might be irrelevant to the evaluation of modern culture. Even as the French poet Charles Baudelaire argued that modern art must be modern, and must reflect its times and be judged by its success in doing so – it should, he suggested, exemplify the "profound harmony" that "controls all the components of history" in a given context – he reiterated his belief in the notion of eternal beauty that had long sustained the claims of the art of the past to exemplarity:

> Beauty is made up of an eternal, invariable element, whose quantity it is excessively difficult to determine, and of a relative, circumstantial element, which will be, if you like, whether severally or all at once, the age, its fashions, its morals, its emotions. Without this second element . . . the first element would be beyond our powers of digestion or appreciation, neither adapted nor suitable to human nature.[1]

The template against which modern art sought to measure itself was above all the art of classical Greece, followed by the successful revival of classical forms under the Renaissance.[2] The heading of one of the early chapters in the German art critic J. J. Winckelmann's enormously influential *History of the Art of Antiquity* of 1764 encapsulates this attitude: "Reasons and causes for the development of Greek art and for its superiority over the art of other peoples." As Winckelmann argued, "the only way for us to become great, and indeed – if this is possible – inimitable, is by imitating the ancients."[3] Hegel, whose philosophical theory of art as simply a reflection of the progressive development of human consciousness might have implied a more sceptical evaluation of Greek achievements, supported this view; classical art was not to be judged solely in terms of its form or technical proficiency, but by the more nebulous notion of its proper content:

> There is certainly among all the world-historical peoples poetry, figurative art, science and philosophy; but they differ not only in style and general tendency but still more in content, and this content concerns the most import-ant difference, that of their rationality . . . One might wish to set the Indian epics on the same level as the Homeric on the basis of a whole mass of formal characteristics . . . but there still remains the infinite difference of content . . . There is not only a classic form, but also a classic content, and moreover form and content in a work of art are so tightly bound together that the one can be classic only insofar as the other is.[4]

In the middle of the nineteenth century, the composer Richard Wagner, a firm believer in the possibility of creating great and inimitable art in the present, not to mention the "art-work of the future," was still in no doubt as to the necessity of looking back to the past in order to do so: "In any serious investigation of the essence of our art today, we cannot make one step forward without being brought face to face with its intimate connection with the *Art of ancient Greece*."[5] However, Wagner also identified the risks of such retrospection, if not tightly controlled by a truly modern creative spirit; modern sculpture was indeed "the expression of an honourable wish to reach back from an unlovely present to the past," but the result was "a mere plagiarism of the genuine art."[6]

Wagner's comment highlights the fact that the deficiencies of modern art and other cultural products were seen primarily as a matter not of their form or content – indeed, a case could be made that modern culture was excessively dependent on the attempted recreation of the artistic forms of the past, rather than creating anything of its own – but of their perceived quality and spirit. The accumulation of ever more detailed and sophisticated understanding of the artistic techniques and subject matter of classical art had proved, contrary to Winckelmann's expectations, manifestly insufficient to inspire great art in the present. At best, an individual genius like the poet Goethe had managed to make something of them, but culture as a whole could not depend solely on the output of isolated individuals, and by the mid-nineteenth century Goethe too belonged to a past whose achievements the present was failing to match.

> Civilization is itself the necessary consequence of the changes which are produced in the volume and density of societies. If science, art and economic activity develop, it is in accordance with a necessity that is imposed upon men. It is because there is, for them, no other way of living in the new conditions in which they have been placed. From the time that the number of individuals among whom social relations are established begins to increase, they can maintain themselves only by greater specialisation, harder work and the intensification of their faculties. From this general stimulation, there inevitably results a much higher degree of culture.[7]

The optimism of Emile Durkheim that progress could not fail to transform all aspects of human life for the better was not widely shared. Had Richard Wagner, Friedrich Nietzsche, or Matthew Arnold had the opportunity to comment on his statement, they would doubtless have dismissed it as the perspective of the "philistine" or the archetypal modern, who simply had no conception of the true meaning of culture and was incapable of evaluating it correctly. For the vast majority of writers who focused on the subject, any consideration of the theme of culture provoked anguish and discontent with modernity for its manifest failure to nurture art and artists. This constituted clear grounds for rejecting smug assumptions of the superiority of the present over the past; moreover, it could be argued that it is the ability of a society to produce great art, not merely its level of material production, that should be taken as the essential criterion of judgment of its achievements. "From the heart of our modern society, from the golden calf of wholesale speculation, stalled at the meeting of its crossroads, our art sucks forth its life-juices": Wagner offers a simultaneous and mutually reinforcing critique of both society and art.[8] The identification of culture as an important object of investigation led writers to stress the connection between society and its cultural products, so that the perceived inadequacies of modern culture formed a basis for the critique of modern values. Further, a stunted, underdeveloped culture could be seen as, at the least, a symptom of the social problems of modernity – if not in fact their cause, as in Schiller's argument that a truly modern society was inconceivable if the people had not previously been made ready to live in it through a process of aesthetic reflection.[9]

Above all, however, the comparison of ancient and modern culture established a problem that had to be addressed: why was it apparently impossible to produce true art – art that could match the achievements of classical antiquity – in a society which otherwise enjoyed every advantage over its predecessors? Theories of the relationship between culture and society offered the possibility of understanding antiquity's success and modernity's failure. Differences between ancient and modern society, or the place of culture in each of these contexts, or the nature of the ancient and the modern individual, might hold the key both to diagnosing the sickness of modern culture and, more importantly, suggesting a remedy.

The complexity of debates on this subject derives to a great extent from the fact that culture was and continues to be an essentially contested concept with multiple definitions. In English, the term can equally well be associated with spiritual or material development, with the general state of cultural and intellectual activity, or with a high level of artistic excellence.[10] "Culture" in its broad definition is often put forward as the determining influence on the cultural products which are frequently taken to define it; that is to say, culture (drama, literature, art) reflects culture (religion, customs, world view). The German concept *Bildung* is equally problematic, as it can refer not only to "education" but also to culture in a more general sense as the intended outcome of the educative process; translators are often compelled to alternate between the two senses within a single text. This tension is developed explicitly in some of Nietzsche's writing, which alternates between denunciations of modern *Bildung* and scepticism as to whether it can be considered true *Bildung* at all, by the standards established by the Greeks:

> If a contemporary man was compelled to return to that world through some enchantment, he would probably consider the Greeks very "uncultivated" – whereupon the so painstakingly disguised secret of modern culture would be uncovered to public laughter; for we moderns have nothing at all of our own; only by filling and over-filling ourselves with alien ages, customs, arts, philosophies, religions and insights do we become anything worthy of attention, namely, walking encyclopedias, which is how an ancient Greek who wound up in our own time would perhaps regard us.[11]

Bildung, as the novelist Thomas Mann was later to suggest, derived from "an insufficiency and sense of discontent when faced with one-sidedness," but its actual modern manifestation could itself come to seem one-sided and thus a further source of discontent with modernity.[12]

> All "culture" appears as man's emancipation from the organically prescribed cycle of natural life. For this very reason every step forward seems condemned to lead to an ever more devastating senselessness. The advancement of cultural values, however, seems to become a senseless bustle in the service of worthless, moreover contradictory, and mutually antagonistic ends.[13]

Underlying all such accounts of the discontent and distress aroused by modern culture is the sense that this should not be the case, that culture should rather bring pleasure and illumination and give meaning to existence, as – it was believed – it had for the Greeks.

The Impossibility of Achilles

> And so one feels ashamed and fearful before the Greeks; unless there may be one who respects the truth above everything and so dares to confess also this truth to himself, that the Greeks hold in their hands the reins of our culture and every other culture, but that almost always the chariot and the horses are made of too poor material and fail to measure up to the

glory of their drivers, who then regard it as a joke to chase such a vehicle into the abyss, which they themselves pass over with the leap of Achilles.

F. Nietzsche, *Die Geburt der Tragödie*, 97–8

The idealization of Greek culture went hand in hand with the critique of modern culture; an emphasis on the special qualities of the former frequently implied the deficiencies of the latter, even when this was not explicitly stated. There was a similarly intimate relationship between attempts at explaining the achievements of the Greeks and diagnoses of the deficiencies of the moderns. It is difficult to read Winckelmann's account of the main characteristics of the Greeks and their society without feeling that this account incorporates a reaction against his own world: the importance of the Mediterranean climate ("much that we might imagine as ideal was natural for them"),[14] their appreciation of physical beauty, and their freedom from the excess of artificial manners, and refinement, and decorum.[15] "In Greece . . . whose inhabitants were dedicated from childhood to joy and delight, and where our present-day criteria of respectability never interfered with the freedom of manners, natural beauty revealed itself naked for the instruction of the artist."[16] Similarly aestheticized images of the Greeks, especially of the young Greek male, recur regularly in later writers. The German philosopher Herder, for example, returned to the idea of classical Greece as the youth of humanity: "the boy has outgrown home and school and stands there – noble youth with beautiful oiled limbs, favourite of all the Graces and lover of the Muses, victor in Olympia and all other games, mind and body together just a single blooming flower."[17] Wagner was one of those who made the contrast between Christian and pagan morality and attitudes to beauty more explicit: "The free Greek, who set himself upon the pinnacle of nature, could procreate art from very joy in manhood . . . Art is the highest expression of activity of a race that has developed its physical beauty in unison with itself and nature."[18] The English critic Matthew Arnold, for all his insistence on the need for "Hellenism" to be tempered with the moral fibre of the "Hebrew" tradition, echoed the same sentiments:

> The best art and poetry of the Greeks, in which religion and poetry are one, in which the idea of beauty and of a human nature perfect on all sides adds to itself a religious and devout energy, and works in the strength of that, is on this account of such surpassing interest and instructiveness for us . . . Greece did not err in having the idea of beauty, harmony and complete human perfection so present and paramount.[19]

These idealizing accounts did not, however, set up a direct, historicized contrast between Greece and modernity, but rather between the Greeks and all other societies, past and present. Further, they seemed to open up the possibility that an individual might be able to recreate within himself something of the spirit of the Greeks, by placing himself in surroundings more conducive to the aesthetic and creative senses (the Mediterranean, above all) and by opening himself to the love of beauty.[20] Goethe made precisely this attempt, but with a clear awareness of its limitations in a modern context:

> Man may achieve much through the purposeful application of isolated faculties, and he may achieve the extraordinary by combining several of his capacities; but he can accomplish the unique, the totally unexpected, only when all his resources are uniformly united within him. The latter was the happy lot of the ancients, especially of the Greeks in their best period; fate has assigned the two former possibilities to the moderns.[21]

The problem was that the individual, as was increasingly recognized, was not wholly free and receptive to classical influences, but was shaped, at least in part, by the conditions of his society. The Greeks could produce great art because they were complete individuals and not alienated from nature; the moderns are not, and so cannot.

In the closing decades of the eighteenth century, this perspective came with an optimistic gloss: the moderns were not *yet* complete individuals, but this possibility seemed within reach as society seemed to be on the brink of transformation. Surveys of modern culture were then intimately connected with the critique of modern social structures, developed through contrast with the idealized society of antiquity. Accounts of Greek art placed particular importance on freedom, echoing the sentiments of Herodotus and other ancient authors that Athens' liberation from tyranny was the root of its success. "Freedom was the chief reason for their art's superiority," argued Winckelmann.[22] Friedrich Schiller's essay *On the Aesthetic Education of Man* is sometimes seen to represent a retreat from the political in response to the excesses and failures of the French Revolution, but it should rather be seen as arguing for the intimate relationship between freedom and culture. For Schiller, it is simply a matter of placing developments in the correct order, as Greek art depends on Greek freedom and institutions, but that freedom depends in turn on the existence of fully developed spirits, nourished by art and the love of beauty.

This diagnosis of modernity's cultural deficiencies highlighted the need for political and social reform, which would be brought about through the promotion of culture. In the middle of the next century, Wagner offered a similar recipe: "True art is highest freedom, and only the highest freedom can bring her forth from herself."[23]

The actual state of modern society, with its lack of freedom, inadequate institutions and slavish spirit, therefore fully explained the state of modern culture; it was remarkable that anything of any merit could be produced under such conditions, and only a genius like Goethe was capable of doing so. Art naturally reflected the condition of one-sided and alienated individuals, the spirit of the people, a divided society, and its utilitarian and material values; it highlighted the extent to which this condition was unnatural and dehumanizing.

> The course of events has given a direction to the spirit of the age which threatens to distance it more and more from the art of the ideal. This art must abandon reality and lift itself with appropriate boldness above necessity; for art is a daughter of freedom, and she must receive her direction from the needs of spirits, not from the exigencies of the material. Today, however, necessity rules, and presses down degraded humanity under its tyrannous yoke. *Utility* is the great idol of the age.[24]

> In the Grecian art and poetry we find an original and unconscious unity of form and subject; in the modern, so far as it has remained true to its own spirit, we observe a keen struggle to unite the two, as being naturally in opposition to one another.[25]

> Our modern stage materialises the ruling spirit of our social life . . . It denotes, to all appearance, the flower of our culture; just as the Grecian tragedy denoted the culminating point of the Greek spirit; but ours is the efflorescence of corruption, of a hollow, soulless and unnatural condition of human affairs and human relations.[26]

This perspective on the relation of modern culture to the modern "spirit" was not confined to the German tradition. Matthew Arnold's *Culture and Anarchy* offered similar ideas, but focused on the way that culture (in the narrow sense) might be able to counteract the tendencies of modern culture as a whole:

> This function [of culture] is particularly important in our modern world, of which the whole civilisation is, to a much greater degree than the

civilisation of Greece and Rome, mechanical and external, and tends constantly to become more so. But above all in our own country has culture a weighty part to perform, because here that mechanical character, which civilisation tends to take everywhere, is shown in the most eminent degree . . . The idea of perfection as an *inward* condition of mind and spirit is at variance with the mechanical and material civilisation in esteem with us.[27]

An alternative explanation for the success of ancient culture was the status of art and of the artist within the *polis*. Nietzsche drew on a long tradition of belief that Athens was an "aesthetic state," and that the Greeks were a people of artists and philosophers, in contrasting the place of creative thought in ancient and modern society:

The task which the philosopher has to perform within a real culture, constituted in a uniform style, cannot be clearly conjectured out of our circumstances and experiences because we have no such culture. On the contrary, only a culture like the Greek can answer the question as to the task of the philosopher, only it can, as I said before, justify philosophy at all, because it alone knows and can make known why and how the philosopher is *not* a chance wanderer, driven randomly here and there. There is a steely necessity which chains the philosopher to a true culture: but how, if this culture does not exist? Then the philosopher is an incalculable and therefore terror-inspiring comet, whereas in the favourable case he shines as the central star in the solar-system of culture.[28]

In the modern world, in contrast, culture is reduced to a private activity, and art is looked down upon as mere handiwork. As Schiller remarked, *à propos* the application of utilitarian judgments of worth to artistic products, "in this clumsy pair of scales the spiritual merit of art has no weight, and, robbed of all encouragement, she removes herself from the clamorous market of this century."[29] Modern culture was founded on an absolute division between the speculative and the business spirit, each one limited and deeply impoverished compared with the harmonious consciousness of the past:

So as the former tries to model the actual on the imaginable, and to raise the subjective conditions of its imagination to the status of laws which establish the existence of things, the latter falls into the opposite extreme of assessing absolutely all experience according to a certain fragment of experience and wishing to apply the rules of its own business to every business without differentiation. The one fell victim to an empty subtlety, the other to a pedantic narrow-mindedness, because one stood too high to see the particular, the other too low to see the whole.[30]

Modern culture was "commercial" or "bourgeois," with everything evaluated in terms of supply, demand, and the needs of the consumer: "This becomes the character of an entire culture, thought through in the minutest and subtlest detail and imprinted in every will and every faculty; it is this of which you men of the coming century will be proud."[31] An equally apocalyptic vision was put forward in England by the arch Platonist and "English pagan," Thomas Taylor:

> We may flourish, indeed, as a commercial people; and stretch the rod of empire over nations as yet unknown . . . but we must remember that the Daemon of commerce is at the same time advancing with giant strides, to trample on the most liberal pursuits, and is preparing with his extended savage arm to crush the votaries of truth and depopulate the divine retreats of philosophy.[32]

The same themes, contrasting the spirit of the ancients and the moderns, echo in Wagner's critique of modern culture.

> The public art of the Greeks, which reached its zenith in their tragedy, was the expression of the deepest and noblest principles of the people's consciousness; with us the deepest and noblest of man's consciousness is the direct opposite of this . . . The Greeks sought the instruments of their art in the products of the highest associate culture; we seek ours in the deepest social barbarism.[33]

> And thus we reach the essential distinction between the two: with the Greeks their public art was indeed art, with us it is artistic handicraft . . .
> The Greek knew no handicraft, rightly so called. The so-called necessities of life – which, strictly speaking, make up the whole concernment of our private and our public life – he deemed unworthy to rank as objects of special and engrossing attention. His soul lived only in public life, in the great fellowship of his nation; the needs of this public life made up the total of his care.[34]

Modern society is simply incapable of supporting art. "Our modern art is a mere product of culture and has not sprung from life itself; therefore, being nothing but a hothouse plant, it cannot strike root in the natural soil or flourish in the natural climate of the present. Art has become the private property of an artist-caste."[35] The only solution is a revolutionary transformation of society, that will sweep away the structures that currently restrict human development and confine the appreciation of art to a privileged elite:

> If he considers the infinitely greater mass of those who are shut out on every side by the evils of our present social system from both the understanding and the tasting of the sweets of modern art, then the artist of today must grow conscious that his whole art-doings are at bottom nothing but an egotistic, self-concerning business; that his art, in the light of private life, is nothing else than luxury and superfluity, a self-amusing pastiche. The daily emphasised and bitterly deplored abyss between so-called culture and un-culture is so enormous; a bridge between the two so inconceivable; a reconciliation so impossible; that, if it had any candour, our modern art . . . would be forced to admit, to its deepest shame, that it owes its existence to a life-element which in turn can base its own existence only on the utter dearth of culture among the real masses of mankind.[36]

An alternative approach to the question of the relation between culture and society was offered by Karl Marx. Cultural questions do not play a great role in his published writings, which treat the world of ideas as a product of the structures of the economy: "the ideas of the ruling class are in every epoch the ruling ideas . . . The class which has the means of material production at its disposal, has control at the same time over the means of mental production, so that thereby, generally speaking, the ideas of those who lack the means of mental production are subject to it."[37] In his notebooks, however, Marx sketched a more nuanced analysis of the incompatibility between classical art and modern development.[38]

> In the case of the arts, it is well known that certain periods of their flowering are out of all proportion to the general development of society, hence also to the material foundation, the skeletal structure as it were, of its organisation. For example, the Greeks compared to the moderns or also Shakespeare. It is even recognised that certain forms of art, e.g. the epic, can no longer be produced in their world epoch-making, classical stature as soon as the production of art, as such, begins; that is, that certain significant forms within the realms of the arts are possible only at an undeveloped stage of artistic development.[39]

Greek art was epoch-making and unsurpassable, not because the Greeks were superior to the moderns but because they were, in material terms, far inferior. Modern progress thus made the classical world view unsustainable.

> It is well known that Greek mythology is not only the arsenal of Greek art but also its foundation. Is the view of nature and of social relations on which the Greek imagination and hence Greek mythology is based possible with self-acting mule spindles and railways and locomotives and electrical telegraphs? What chance has Vulcan against Roberts & Co., Jupiter against the lightning-rod and Hermes against the Crédit Mobilier? All mythology overcomes and dominates and shapes the forces of nature in the imagination and by the imagination; it therefore vanishes with the advent of real mastery over them. What becomes of Fama alongside Printing House Square? Greek art presupposes Greek mythology, i.e. nature and the social forms already reworked in an unconsciously artistic way by the popular imagination . . . Is Achilles possible with powder and lead? Or the *Iliad* with the printing press, not to mention the printing machine? Do not the song and the saga and the muse necessarily come to an end with the printer's bar, hence do not the necessary conditions of epic poetry vanish?[40]

Art, for Marx, reflects the world that produces it; not in the crude sense of reproducing class antagonisms in the field of mental production, but rather in the sense that art is inspired by the conditions of existence of individuals and their relation to the world. Greek art was not the product of individual genius but of the world view of a particular society; it presupposed a particular mythology – Egyptian mythology could never have supported it – "but in any case a *mythology*. Hence in no way a social development which excludes all mythological, all mythologising relations to nature; which therefore demands of the artist an imagination not dependent on mythology."[41]

Disenchantment and Decadence

The idea that the modern world has been demythologized, with serious consequences for the production of art, was not original to Marx. It is a key theme in Schiller's writings, including his 1788 poem *Die Götter Griechenlands*, contrasting ancient and modern understanding of the natural world. "Where now, as our wise men tell us, a ball of fire revolves soullessly, then Helios drove his golden chariot in silent majesty"; "Of those warm and living images, only the skeleton remains behind for me"; "Like the dead beating of the pendulum clock, de-godded Nature serves them, subservient to the law of gravity"; "Leisurely the gods return home to the poet's land, useless to a world which, too grown up for leading-strings, holds itself in balance by itself."[42] Emancipation from the power of nature, both in fact and in imagination, had been achieved by modernity, but at a clear cost; the world is now joyless and lifeless, and, while only art offers any hope of transcending this reality, the lack of beauty and enchantment in the world make it difficult to find any inspiration except in the lost past of classical antiquity. Now, as Schiller argued in *The Aesthetic Education of Man*, the process had gone too far, and yet seemed to be unstoppable. "The philosophical spirit of enquiry seizes one province after another from the imagination, and the frontiers of art are contracted, the more that science expands its boundaries."[43] Not only were science and philosophy destroying the basis of the artistic view of nature, they were undermining art itself. The drive to analyze and understand culture in a scientific manner cannot serve as the basis for a living art:

> Unfortunately understanding must first destroy the object of the inner sense if it wishes to make it its own. Like the chemist, the philosopher can find unity only by breaking things into their separate elements, and the work of spontaneous nature only through the torture of art. In order to catch the fleeting appearance he must bind it in the shackles of rules, dissect its beautiful body into concepts, and preserve its living spirit in a meagre word-skeleton. Is it any wonder if natural feeling does not recognise itself in such a likeness?[44]

One of the recurring themes in Schiller's writings is the importance of "naturalness" of feeling, above all in the contrast he developed between "naïve" and "sentimental" poetry – the former exemplified of course by the natural, unselfconscious genius of the Greeks, the latter by the painfully constructed, inferior products of the moderns. "They felt naturally; we feel the natural."[45] "The feeling of which we here speak is therefore not that which the ancients possessed; it is rather identical with that which *we have for the ancients*."[46] Similar ideas were developed by Hegel, discussing the differences between ancient and modern historiography: "our culture is essentially interpretative and immediately transforms all events into reports for intellectual appreciation."[47]

The development of reflection in our life today has made it a need of ours, in relation both to our will and judgement, to cling to general considerations and to regulate the particular by them . . . But for artistic interest and production we demand in general rather a quality of life in which the universal is not present in the form of law and maxim, but which gives the impression of being one with the senses and the feelings . . . Consequently the conditions of our present time are not favourable to art.[48]

Hegel compared the ancient understanding of a cult statue as the actual abode of a god with the modern view of it as (merely) a work of art, exemplifying the contrast between the externality of the Greeks and the inwardness of the moderns:

The statues are now mere corpses from which the living soul has flown, just as the hymns are words from which belief has gone. The tables of the gods provide no spiritual food and drink, and in his games and festivals man no longer recovers the joyful consciousness of his unity with the divine. The works of the muse now lack the power of the spirit, for the spirit has gained certainty of itself from the crushing of gods and men. They have become what they are for us now – beautiful fruit already picked from the tree, which a friendly fate has offered us, as a girl might set the fruit before us.[49]

"In all these respects, art, considered in its highest vocation, is and remains for us a thing of the past."[50] Modern art is lifeless because of the loss of naturalness; however, classical art is also lifeless *to us*, whether because of the distance between now and then or because of the contrast between the spirit of its reception and that of its creation. "Beauty, too, is now only one of our abstract notions," argued Wagner, "and indeed no notion deduced from actual life, but from Greek art turned into a lesson."[51] For Nietzsche, "the critical-historical spirit of our education" was responsible for destroying myth – without which "every culture loses its healthy, creative, natural energy" – as modern man could believe in its former importance "only by following scholarly approaches, through mediating abstractions."[52] Nietzsche speaks of the "eternal struggle between the *theoretical* and the *tragic views of the world*"; "Whoever recalls the immediate effects produced by this spirit of science, restlessly driving forwards, will recognise at once how *myth* was destroyed by it, and how through this destruction poetry was driven from its natural, ideal soil, and henceforth is homeless."[53] Attempts at drawing inspiration from modernity in the way that the Greeks had been inspired by their world were clearly fruitless:

> Then we find the demand that from time to time an image or a metaphor should appear, that the metaphor must however be new; "new" and "modern" are, however, for the inadequate writerly brain the same thing, and now it torments itself to draw its metaphors from the railway, the telegraph, the steam-engine, the stock exchange, and feels proud that the images must be new because they are modern.[54]

For Weber, heavily influenced by Nietzsche's arguments, a fundamental distinction between modern and pre-modern cultures was the status accorded to the "specialist" rather than the "cultivated man" in society, and the resultant orientation of educational systems.[55] Ancient education had long been held up as a model for the present – albeit on widely diverging grounds, as Rousseau claimed that it demonstrated the necessity of state education to form citizens and Adam Smith cited it in opposition to any form of publicly organized or publicly funded education.[56] Comte too had focused on the social implications of specialization in education, in science and culture as much as in the economy:

> We may find something quite as lamentable in the intellectual class, in the exclusive employment of a human brain in resolving some equations, or in classifying insects. The moral effect is, unhappily, analogous in the two cases. It occasions a miserable indifference about the general course of human affairs, as long as there are equations to resolve or pins to manufacture.[57]

Weber, however, was concerned rather with the way that education reflected broader social processes; ancient education aimed at developing "cultivation" because that was what was required for the exercise of power in a patriarchal, pre-rationalized society, whereas the technocratic and bureaucratized modern world requires experts. Rationalization of society and education does not give individuals greater knowledge of the conditions of life, such as the operation of a tram or the workings of a monetary economy, but it gives them "the knowledge or belief that if one but wished one *could* learn it at any time":

> Hence it means that principally there are no mysterious incalculable forces that come into play, but rather that one can, in principle, master all things by calculation. This means that the world is disenchanted. One need no

longer have recourse to magical means in order to master or implore the spirits, as did the savage, for whom such mysterious powers existed. Technical means and calculations perform the service.[58]

This, for Weber, is the world view characteristic of modernity: demythologized, scientific, separated from nature and convinced of its mastery of the world. This has serious implications for cultural activity. Weber drew a sharp contrast between the artistic experimenters of the Renaissance, for whom "science meant the path to true art, and that meant for them the path to true nature," and the modern perception that science and art, science and nature were in absolute opposition; the goal today is "redemption from the intellectualisation of science in order to return to one's own nature and therewith to nature in general." Rationalization had advanced beyond what humanity could bear; science had been shown to be inadequate as a replacement for traditional beliefs as a means of making sense of the world: "If these natural sciences lead to anything in this way, they are apt to make the belief that there is any such thing as the 'meaning' of the universe die out at its very roots."[59]

There was of course an obvious difficulty in contrasting natural Greeks, ruled by feelings and inspired by mythology, with the rational, scientific moderns; the Greeks also needed to be set forward as the pioneering philosophers and lovers of reason, in contrast, if not in direct opposition, to the superstitions of Christianity. For Winckelmann, the Greeks had been thinkers as much as athletes and artists:

> Greeks in their prime were contemplative beings; they were already thinking twenty years or more before we generally begin to think for ourselves, and they exercised the mind when it was most fired up by the sprightliness of the body, whereas with us the mind is ignobly nourished until it decays.[60]

In Matthew Arnold's *Culture and Anarchy*, the Greeks exemplify rationality and intellectual curiosity in contrast to the legalistic morality of the Hebrews. "The uppermost idea with Hellenism is to see things as they really are . . . The Greek quarrel with the body and its desires is that they hinder right thinking."[61]

> Greek intelligence has obviously for its essence the instinct for what Plato calls the true, firm, intelligible law of things: the law of light, of seeing things as they are. Even in the natural sciences, where the Greeks had not time

and means adequately to apply this instinct, and where we have gone a great deal further than they did, it is this instinct which is the root of the whole matter and the ground of all our success; and this instinct the world has mainly learnt of the Greeks, inasmuch as they are humanity's most signal manifestation of it.[62]

Arnold's theme is the necessity of striking a balance, appropriate to the age, between the instincts of Hellenes and Hebrews. At the close of antiquity, humanity had been unable to live up to the demands of Hellenism; human nature had been insufficiently gentle, simple, and noble, so that the Hebraism of St Paul and Christianity better met its needs. Now that they had learnt discipline and hard work, however, people needed to take back on board the virtues taught by the Greeks. To some extent the Greeks become moderns, as they had been in the previous century, standing for the exercise of human reason against superstition and custom; however, in Arnold's view the moderns have an opportunity to lift themselves to a higher level because they can continue to draw upon the legacy of Hebraism:

> Both Hellenism and Hebraism arise out of the wants of human nature, and address themselves to satisfying those wants. But their methods are so different, they lay stress on such different points, and call into being by their respective disciplines such different activities, that the face which human nature presents when it passes from the hands of one of them to those of the other is no longer the same.[63]

Friedrich Nietzsche also focused on the relationship between the values of antiquity and Christianity as the key to the cultural failings of modernity. From his perspective, there could be no possibility of striking a balance with the "sickness" of Christianity: Christian values were precisely what had to be destroyed – or revalued – in order to free human creativity from its fetters. However, Christianity was not the only problem; in important respects, the intellectual difficulties and dilemmas of modernity could be traced further back, to antiquity itself:

> Our whole modern world is caught in the net of Alexandrian culture, and knows as its ideal the *theoretical man*, equipped with the highest powers of understanding and working in the service of science, whose archetype and progenitor is Socrates.[64]

The central modern drama of the incompatibility of art and the scientific spirit, Nietzsche argued, had long since been played out, back in the fifth century BCE.

> There are periods in which the man of reason and the man of intuition stand next to one another, the one fearful of intuition, the other filled with scorn for abstraction; the latter as unreasonable as the former is inartistic. Both desire to rule over life . . . Where the man of intuition, as in ancient Greece, wields his weapons more powerfully and victoriously than his opposite, in favourable conditions a culture can take shape, and the rule of art over life can become established.[65]

The heart of Nietzsche's argument is less about the birth than the death of tragedy, in the face of the triumph of reason over intuition. "That which brought about the death of tragedy, Socratism in ethics, the dialectic, smugness and cheerfulness of theoretical man – what? could not exactly this Socratism be a sign of decline, of exhaustion, of sickness, of the anarchic dissolution of the instincts?"[66] Modern culture is merely the culmination of a long process of the destruction of the illusions that are essential for any culture to exist; its main symptoms are the results of the belief that reason and science, rather than art, can give life meaning:

> It is the mark of that "rupture," which everyone is accustomed to say is the original ailment of modern culture, that theoretical man shrinks back from his own consequences and, discontented, no longer dares to trust himself to the terrifying ice-stream of existence; fearfully he runs up and down the bank . . . He feels that a culture which is founded on the principle of science must collapse if it begins to become *illogical*, i.e. to flee from its own consequences. Our art manifests this general affliction; all for nothing that one relies, in an imitative manner, on all the great productive periods and natures, all for nothing that one gathers the whole of "world literature" around modern man as a consolation and places him in the middle of all the artistic styles and artists of every time . . . He remains still the eternally hungered, the "critic" without desire or strength, the Alexandrian man, who is at bottom a librarian and proof-reader and ruins his eyesight miserably with book-dust and printing errors.[67]

"Our modern culture is not a living thing . . . It is not a real culture at all but only a kind of knowledge of culture; there remains in it something of an idea of culture and a feeling for culture, but no cultural achievement results from this."[68] This condition is exemplified for Nietzsche in the

modern study of classical antiquity and the place of the classics in education, precisely because this highlights the yawning gulf between the
cultures of antiquity and modernity.

> That one can attain culture only through antiquity is not true. But one
> *can* attain it through that route. Culture as one currently understands it,
> no. Our culture is built upon a wholly castrated and mendacious study of
> antiquity. In order to see how ineffective this study is, one simply looks at
> the philologists: they ought to be the most highly cultivated men through
> antiquity.[69]

Clearly that is not the case. On the contrary, knowledge of antiquity is
acquired by modern philologists simply as knowledge for its own sake,
not as something that should transform one's life and one's view of the
world. "Our philologists stand in the same relation to real educators as
the medicine-men of the savages do to real doctors. How a distant time
will marvel at us!"[70] "They lack the real desire for the strong and
powerful traits of antiquity. They become eulogists and thereby become
ridiculous."[71] "I think that 99 out of 100 philologists *shouldn't* be."[72] For
Nietzsche, the philologist is the archetypal modern, exemplifying all the
faults of modern culture.[73]

> The proud conceit of our classics teachers goes so far in imagining that
> they are as it were *in possession of the ancients* that they transfer this
> arrogance to their pupils, together with the suspicion that such a posses-
> sion, while it certainly does not make us happy, is good enough for poor,
> foolish, honest old book-dragons.[74]

The absolute inferiority of modern culture is exemplified in its attempted
appropriation of antiquity, its naïve belief that through science and reason
it has mastered and surpassed the Greeks, while in fact missing the point
entirely. Modern belief in the possibility of reviving the Greeks, and modern
belief that antiquity has been overcome and surpassed, are equally ridiculous: they demonstrate the decadence of reason in its proud illusion of
mastery, and the decadence of classical philology in its failure to recognize
the vast, unbridgeable gulf that lay between antiquity and modernity.

> There is no other artistic period in which so-called cultured education and
> actual art have with such estrangement and dislike confronted one another,
> than that which we see before our eyes in the present. We understand why

such a feeble culture hates true art; for it fears its own destruction as a result. But might not a whole type of culture, namely the Socratic–Alexandrian, have lived itself out, now that it has resulted in such a slight and dainty peak as present-day education? If such heroes as Goethe and Schiller could not succeed in breaking through the enchanted gateway which leads into the Hellenic magic mountain . . . what remains for the epigones ["successors"] of such heroes to hope for?[75]

On Being an Epigone

In his notes in the *Grundrisse*, Marx had proved to his own satisfaction why it was impossible to recreate Greek art in the modern world, but this was not the end of the story. "The difficulty is that they still afford us artistic pleasure, and that in a certain respect they count as a norm and as an unattainable model." This was both a puzzle and a problem. Why did the art of an "undeveloped" stage of society continue to appeal to a society whose material conditions and conception of the world were quite different? Further, how should one respond to the sense of loss and inadequacy that this situation created? Marx's answer to the first of these problems was threefold: firstly, that the Greeks had produced something of "world epoch-making, classical stature" that transcended the limitations of their time; secondly, that it was quite natural for the "historic childhood of humanity, its most beautiful unfolding" to exercise "an eternal charm"; thirdly, that part of this attraction was, as with nostalgia for one's own childhood, precisely the contrast with the present. "The charm of their art for us is not in contradiction to the undeveloped stage of society on which it grew. It is its result, rather, and is inextricably bound up with the fact that the unripe social conditions under which it arose, and could alone arise, can never return." The challenge was to accept the irrevocable loss of the world that had produced such art, to recognize the nature of the changes that had brought this about, and to strive "to reproduce its truth at a higher stage."[76]

Greek culture was, for many writers in the nineteenth century, a problem and a provocation as much as an inspiration. It offered a clear basis for the critique of modern society, undermining modernity's claims to superiority since it had manifestly failed to produce anything of equivalent worth; however, it also represented a source of despair at the impossibility of returning to the pre-modern conditions and state of mind that had made Greek culture possible. Attempts at responding to this feeling of dissatisfaction by analyzing the reasons for modernity's failure ran the risk of accentuating it by emphasizing the gulf that separated the present from the past. How could one return to the world of myth now that science had revealed it to be illusion? How could one escape the iron cage of modern rationality without becoming irrational? As Marx put it, "a man cannot become a child again, or he becomes childish."[77] But that left the Greeks, those precocious children and sophisticated primitives, as a permanent challenge to the values and illusions of demythologized, rationalized and cultureless modernity.

> It must be stated that the influence of Socrates, has spread out across the world that followed him, up to this moment and far into the future, like a shadow growing ever larger in the evening sun, requiring the new creation of *art* again and again, art in its already metaphysical, widest and deepest sense . . . Before this could be recognised, before the innermost dependence of all art on the Greeks, the Greeks from Homer to Socrates, was convincingly set forth, it was necessary for us to experience these Greeks as the Athenians did Socrates. Almost every period and stage of culture has tried at some point to free itself with deep resentment from the Greeks, because in comparison with them all one's own achievements, apparently completely original and sincerely admired, suddenly seemed to lose colour and life and shrank into unsuccessful copies or even caricature.[78]

Three different responses to this problem can be identified. The first was the optimistic belief that modernity could be reinvigorated or civilized through a suitable infusion of the Hellenic spirit, to restore the natural balance between "knowing" and "doing": "Now, and for us, it is a time to Hellenise, and to praise knowing; for we have Hebraized too much, and have over-valued doing."[79] Matthew Arnold emphasized the need for compromise and balance: "In its blame of Hebraising too, and in its praise of Hellenising, culture must not fail to keep its flexibility, and to give to its judgements that passing and provisional character which we have seen it impose on its preferences and rejections of machinery."[80] He argued forcefully for the power of culture to create a frame of mind that would be conducive to reforming society and promoting the idea of equality:

> "Would any amount of wealth be worth having with the condition that one was to become just like these people by having it?" And thus culture begets a dissatisfaction which is of the highest possible value in stemming

the common tide of men's thoughts in a wealthy and industrial community, and which saves the future, as one may hope, from being vulgarised, even if it cannot save the present.[81]

Culture looks beyond machinery, culture hates hatred; culture has one great passion, the passion for sweetness and light. It has one even yet greater – the passion for making them *prevail*. It is not satisfied until we *all* come to a perfect man: it know that the sweetness and light of the few must be imperfect until the raw and unkindled masses of humanity are touched with sweetness and light.[82]

The importance of the Greeks in this project is, rather oddly, both as the epitome of the Hellenic spirit which needs to be restored to its rightful place in modern culture and as the example of the compromise that is required between knowing and doing, the moral and the intellectual, Hellenizing and Hebraizing:

The Greeks – the great exponents of humanity's bent for sweetness and light united, of its perception that the truth of things must be at the same time beauty – singularly escaped the fanaticism which we moderns, whether we Hellenise or whether we Hebraise, are so apt to show. They arrived – though failing, as has been said, to give adequate practical satisfaction to the claims of man's moral side – at the idea of a comprehensive adjustment of the claims of both the sides in man, the moral as well as the intellectual, of a full estimate of both, and of a reconciliation of both; an idea which is philosophically of the greatest value, and the best of lessons for us moderns.[83]

Arnold sees a measured infusion of the spirit of the Greeks as a means of reforming modern culture and hence modern society. A rather more radical approach argued for the reinvention of the spirit of the Greeks for a new epoch, learning the lessons from their experience and drawing on their works more as an inspiration than a direct model, as a means of overcoming rather than improving modernity. This argument could be offered as grounds for a rejection of the pursuit of culture altogether in favor of the promotion of civic virtue, as Rousseau suggested on the basis of the Spartan example and the awful warning of Athens: "the progress of the Arts, the disintegration of morals, and the Macedonian's yoke closely followed one another."[84] Far more common, however, was the vision offered by Goethe, Schiller, and other romantic Hellenists of the transformative potential of true culture.

Schiller elaborates the argument in detail. "Indeed, nothing is more usual, than for both science and art to embrace the spirit of the age, and for creative taste to welcome the law of critical judgement" – with deleterious consequences.[85] However, the artist can escape the pernicious influence of the spirit of modern society through a return to the Greeks as a source of transcendental ideals and artistic forms, antipathetic to the modern.

> The artist is certainly the child of his time; but it is the worse for him if he is also its pupil, let alone its favourite. May some charitable deity snatch the infant from his mother's breast, nourish him with the milk of a better age and let him ripen to maturity under a distant Grecian sky. When he has then become a man, he returns, an alien figure, to his own century; but not to gladden it by its appearance, but, terrifying as Agamemnon's son, to cleanse it. He will indeed take his material from the present, but borrow his artistic forms from a nobler time, indeed from beyond all time, from the absolute unchangeable unity of his being. Here, out of the pure aether of his daemonic nature, flows the source of beauty, untainted by the corruption of the generations and ages which wallow in muddy eddies far below.[86]

"Truth lives on in the midst of deception" – the ability of classical forms to inspire reverence, even in the midst of the depravities of the Roman Empire, shows this – "and from the copy the original will once again be restored."[87] The artist can concentrate his efforts "through the union of the possible with the necessary, to produce the ideal,"[88] an art which then works on modernity by rekindling the love of beauty, affinity for art, and sense of play. The Greek example offers a new understanding of what it ought to mean to be human:

> We shall never be wrong in seeking a man's ideal of beauty along the same path in which he satisfies his play impulse . . . For, to declare it once and for all, man plays only when he is in the full sense of the word a man, and he is only wholly man when he is playing. This proposition, which at the moment perhaps seems paradoxical, will assume great and deep significance when we have once reached the point of applying it to the twofold seriousness of duty and of destiny; it will, I promise you, support the whole fabric of aesthetic art, and the still more difficult art of living. But it is only in science that this statement is unexpected; it has long since been alive and operative in art, and in the feeling of the Greeks, its most distinguished exponents; only they transferred to Olympus what should have been realized on earth.[89]

The return to the Greeks offers, for Schiller, the possibility of surpassing the Greeks; the freedom and leisure to enjoy culture, which they reserved for a few, would be extended to the whole of humanity in the new society which will be brought into being when men's minds have been transformed through art.

The third response was to take the opposite approach for the same motives: the rejection of any attempt at imitating the Greeks in the interests of a revolutionary transformation of society through an art appropriate to its times. From this viewpoint, the historical perspective reveals not only the brilliance but also the limitations of Greek culture; it was necessary to learn from their mistakes, to build something better and more lasting:

> No, we do not wish to revert to Greekness: for what the Greeks did not know, and, not knowing it, came to their downfall – this *we* know. It is their very fall, whose cause we now perceive after years of misery and deepest universal suffering, that shows us clearly what we should become; it shows us that we must love all men before we can rightly love ourselves, before we can regain true joy in our own personality. From the dishonouring slave-yoke of universal journeyman-hood with its sickly money-soul we wish to soar to the free manhood of art, with the star-rays of its world-soul; from the weary, over-burdened day-labourers of commerce we desire to grow to fair strong men, to whom the world belongs as an eternal, inexhaustible source of the highest delights of art.[90]

Wagner's project is remarkably close to Schiller's, with a similar vision of the recreation of the spirit of the Greeks in a society that extends the benefits of culture to all. Where he differed was in his proposed methods, insisting on the limitations and inadequacies of classical forms to encompass modern content. "The foolish restoration of a sham Greek mode of art has been attempted already," he noted, "but nothing better than an inane patchwork could ever come of it"; it evinced the same lifeless abstraction and purely intellectual understanding of art that permeated modern culture. "In our 'climate' the imitated plastic art of Greece can only be a hothouse growth and not a natural plant."[91] The English poet and essayist Samuel Taylor Coleridge had developed a similar argument about the imitation of the antique in sculpture: "it induces an effort to combine together two incongruous things, that is to say, modern feelings in antique forms . . . It speaks in a language, as it were, learned and dead, the tones of which, being unfamiliar, leave the common spectator cold and unimpressed."[92]

For Wagner, "only revolution, not slavish restoration, can give us back that highest art-work" known from Greece.[93] Classical art was a pinnacle of human achievement, but it was also innately conservative – both in its original context, since it perfectly expressed the spirit of the people, and still more in the modern world; for modernity, "true art is revolutionary, because its very existence is opposed to the ruling spirit of the community."[94] The impossibility of returning to classical art "in no way proves that, in our climate, an art could not unfold itself in answer to our veritable human needs."[95] To create the Art-work of the Future, "we have to turn Hellenic art to Human art: to loose from it the stipulations by which it was but a Hellenic art and not a universal art."[96]

One of Wagner's key insights, acknowledged by Nietzsche in *Birth of Tragedy*, was that the notion of the classical in aesthetic terms had been defined above all in the light of sculpture and poetry. In the field of music, he was free to innovate in form, drawing on material more directly related to Germanic traditions, and yet still claim to be inspired by the spirit of the Greeks and their view of how art should relate to society. As Nietzsche argued, this alone seemed to offer any hope of overcoming what otherwise appeared to be the fixed and immovable conditions of modern life:

> Let no one seek to undermine us in our belief in an imminent rebirth of Hellenic antiquity; for in that alone we find our hope for a renewal and cleansing of the German spirit through the fire-magic of music. What would we otherwise know to say, what could otherwise in the desolation and exhaustion of contemporary culture awaken any comforting expectation for the future? In vain we look for a single strongly-sprouting root, for a patch of fertile and healthy soil; everywhere dust, sand, petrification, desiccation.[97]

However, even in his early work, Nietzsche went much further in questioning the dominance of the classical ideal in the name of the Greeks themselves. Rejecting and ironizing the stereotypes inherited from Winckelmann, he sought to establish a different idea of the essence of what it was to be Greek.[98]

> To sniff out in the Greeks "beautiful souls," "golden means" and other perfections, to admire in them their peace in greatness, their ideal disposition and their high simplicity – from this "high simplicity," a *niaiserie allemande* when all is said and done, I was preserved through the psychologist

whom I carry inside me. I saw their strongest instinct, the will to power, I saw them tremble before the unrestrained violence of this drive – I saw all their institutions develop out of precautionary rules in order to make themselves secure against the *explosives* inside them. The immense internal tension discharged itself in terrible and reckless hostility against others; the city communities tore one another to pieces so that each individual citizen could find peace in himself. One simply had to be strong; danger was nearby – it lay in wait everywhere. The magnificent supple physique, the bold realism and immoralism which is peculiar to the Hellene was a necessity, not a "natural quality." It was a consequence, it was not there from the beginning.[99]

Nietzsche identified the decadence of tragedy already in the fifth century BCE, the period of Greek history idealized by every other commentator. The more that the true essence of tragedy was located instead in the archaic, pre-classical past, the more that modern classicism and aestheticism were revealed as the projections of modern longing and dissatisfaction, simply the other side of the coin of modernity's relentless intellectualization and rationalization.[100] Modernity demonstrates its lack of culture through its compulsion to look to other periods for inspiration and materials; it lacks everything that would make it possible even to begin building a real culture. Schiller and Arnold are thus revealed as absurdly optimistic and deluded, since they seek to reform or transform modernity from within without recognizing its true limitations, and to build on an idea of antiquity which is in fact quintessentially modern.

Think of a culture which has no secure and sacred place of origin, but which is condemned to exhaust every possibility and to nourish itself meagrely from all other cultures – that is the present, the result of Socratism directed towards the destruction of myth. Now mythless man stands there, eternally hungry, amidst all the pasts, and, digging and scrabbling, seeks for roots, even if he has to dig for them in the most distant antiquities. What does the enormous historical need of discontented modern culture, the accumulation of countless other cultures and the consuming desire for knowledge point to, if not to the loss of myth, the loss of the mythical home, the mythical maternal womb? One asks whether the feverish and so uncanny agitation of this culture is anything other than the greedy grabbing and nourishment-chasing of the hungry – and who would wish to give anything more to such a culture, which is not to be satisfied by anything which it devours, and contact with which usually transforms the strongest, healthiest food into "History and Criticism"?[101]

The confrontation of ancient and modern culture is more than enough to reveal the limitations of the latter, and to provide a diagnosis of its sickness. However, neither the imitation, inevitably scholarly and intellectualized, of classical forms, nor the attempted recreation of a modern idea of the classical spirit, can offer an escape from the culture of modernity. Rather, classical culture, and modernity's inability to develop a healthy relationship with it, is precisely the problem.

Notes

1   Baudelaire, "Painter of modern life," 3.
2   Marchand (1996), 6.
3   "Thoughts on the imitation of the painting and sculpture of the Greeks," 33.
4   *Vorlesungen über die Philosophie der Geschichte*, 94.
5   Wagner, *Art and Revolution*, 32.
6   *Art-Work of the Future*, 171.
7   Durkheim, *Division of Labour*, 121.
8   *Art and Revolution*, 42.
9   Kain (1982), 15–19; Yack (1992), 133–84.
10 Williams (1983), 89–90.
11 *Vom Nutzen und Nachtheil der Historie*, 273–4.
12 "Reflections of an unpolitical man," 505.
13 Weber, "Religious rejections," 356–7.
14 *History of the Art of Antiquity*, 186.
15 Potts (1994); Marchand (1996), 7–16.
16 Winckelmann, "Thoughts on the imitation," 35.
17 *This Too A Philosophy*, 286.
18 *Art and Revolution*, 38.
19 *Culture and Anarchy*, 54–5.
20 Cf. Trevelyan (1981).
21 Goethe, "Winckelmann," 237.
22 *History of the Art of Antiquity*, 187.
23 *Art and Revolution*, 35.
24 Schiller, *Über der ästhetische Erziehung*, 2.3.
25 Schlegel, *Lectures*, I.214–15.
26 Wagner, *Art and Revolution*, 43.
27 *Culture and Anarchy*, 49.
28 "Die Philosophie im tragischen Zeitalter der Griechen," 809.
29 *Über der ästhetische Erziehung*, 2.3.

30 Ibid., 6.10.
31 Nietzsche, *Daybreak*, no. 175.
32 *The Mystical Initiations*, 187.
33 *Art and Revolution*, 47.
34 Ibid., 49.
35 Wagner, *Art-Work of the Future*, 182.
36 Ibid., 182–3.
37 *German Ideology*, 59.
38 Sannwald (1957), 159–203; Müller (1972).
39 *Grundrisse*, 110.
40 Ibid., 110–11.
41 Ibid., 111.
42 "Die Götter Griechenlands," lines 17–20, 151–2, 166–8, 173–6, in *Gedichte*, 190–5.
43 *Über der ästhetische Erziehung*, 2.3.
44 Ibid., 1.4.
45 "On naïve and sentimental poetry," 190.
46 Ibid.
47 *Vorlesungen über die Philosophie der Geschichte*, 14.
48 *Aesthetics*, 10.
49 *Phenomenology*, 455–6.
50 Hegel, *Aesthetics*, 11.
51 "Art and climate," 263.
52 *Die Geburt der Tragödie*, 145.
53 Ibid., 111.
54 *David Strauss*, 223.
55 *Economy and Society*, 1001–2.
56 Rousseau, *Discourse on Political Economy*, 20, 22; Smith, *Wealth of Nations*, V.i.f.
57 Comte, *Positive Philosophy*, II, 144.
58 'Science as a vocation," 139.
59 Ibid., 142.
60 *History of the Art of Antiquity*, 188.
61 *Culture and Anarchy*, 131.
62 Ibid., 147–8.
63 Ibid., 134.
64 *Die Geburt der Tragödie*, 116.
65 "Über Wahrheit und Lüge im aussermoralischen Sinne," 889.
66 1886 Preface to *Die Geburt der Tragödie*, 12.
67 *Die Geburt der Tragödie*, 119–20.
68 *Vom Nutzen und Nachtheil der Historie*, 273.
69 *Wir Philologen*, 95.

70 Ibid., 160–1.
71 Ibid., 102.
72 Ibid., 96.
73 Porter (2000a).
74 Nietzsche, *Daybreak*, no. 195.
75 Nietzsche, *Die Geburt der Tragödie*, 130–1.
76 *Grundrisse*, 111.
77 Ibid.
78 Nietzsche, *Die Geburt der Tragödie*, 97.
79 Arnold, *Culture and Anarchy*, 37.
80 Ibid.
81 Ibid., 52.
82 Ibid., 69.
83 Ibid., 148–9.
84 *Discourse on the Sciences and Arts*, 18.
85 *Über der ästhetische Erziehung*, 9.3.
86 Ibid., 9.4.
87 Ibid., 9.4 n.87.
88 Ibid., 9.5 n.88.
89 Ibid., 15.8–9.
90 Wagner, *Art and Revolution*, 54.
91 "Art and climate," 258.
92 *A Course of Lectures*, XIII.334.
93 *Art and Revolution*, 53.
94 Ibid., 51–2.
95 "Art and climate," 258.
96 *Art-Work of the Future*, 90.
97 *Die Geburt der Tragödie*, 131.
98 Marchand (1996), 124–8.
99 Nietzsche, *Götzen-Dämmerung*, 157.
100 Porter (2000b).
101 Nietzsche, *Die Geburt der Tragödie*, 146.

5

History as Nightmare

Conceptions of Progress
and Decline

Flight out of reality to the past; whether thereby the conception of antiquity
is falsified?

F. Nietzsche, *Wir Philologen*, 95

Historical study, like economics or sociology, was another field of human
endeavor in which the moderns acknowledged a limited debt to antiquity
but believed themselves to have gone much further in developing human
understanding. Hegel, for example, presented a brief history of the
development of the subject as both a chronological and an intellectual
progression from original to reflective and finally to philosophic history,
with classical historians placed at the beginning (Herodotus, Thucydides,
and Polybius cited as writers of original history and Livy and Diodorus
Siculus representing one form of reflective history), modern historians
located firmly within the reflective category, and his own work figured
as the culmination, alone capable of properly comprehending the true
nature of world-historical development.[1] As in his analysis of other fields
of cultural and intellectual activity, however, Hegel also insisted on the
existence of significant contrasts between classical antiquity and other pre-
modern societies; India is said to have produced no history, while China,
for all its excellent historical records, was not the starting-point for the
development of modern critical and philosophical reflection on the past
but a dead end, simply supplying the raw materials for western historians
to comprehend the unique nature of the modern development.

Other writers offered a similar account; the moderns had surpassed
them, but the ancients – Tacitus and Livy in the Renaissance, succeeded
by Polybius and above all Thucydides in the course of the eighteenth

century – were seen as the founders of the western tradition of history. They constituted a model for critical historiography, not merely recounting events but seeking their causes and meaning, a project which was now being fully developed by modern historians.[2] The programmatic statements of Tacitus and Thucydides on the historian's aims, methodologies and duties were cited almost religiously.[3] The key figure in the development of "scientific history" in Germany in the nineteenth century, Leopold von Ranke, wrote his doctoral dissertation (sadly lost) on Thucydides; the influence of the latter's ideas, of history as a "possession for ever" as a result of its lessons on how men and states behave, and of the historian's duty to evaluate sources on the basis of reason and probability – however easy it may be to identify a gap between the modern interpretation of these precepts and ancient practice – was far-reaching.[4] Friedrich Nietzsche's praise of Thucydides was expressed as ever in idiosyncratic terms, and the contrast with Plato was entirely his own, but the general tenor – the Greek historian as the archetypal detached, analytical observer of human behavior – was entirely conventional for the time.[5]

> My recuperation, my predeliction, my *cure* from all Platonism was Thucydides every time. Thucydides and, perhaps, Machiavelli's Prince are my close kindred because of their absolute determination to pre-judge nothing and to see reason in *reality*, not in "reason," still less in "morality" . . . Nothing cures us more thoroughly of the wretched habit of the Greeks of glossing things over in the ideal, a habit which the "classically educated" youth carries with him into life as the reward for his gymnasium training, than Thucydides. One must turn him over line by line and read his unspoken thoughts as clearly as his words; there is scarcely another thinker with so many hidden thoughts.[6]

Modern historiography's claim to attention was to have elevated the principles of the greatest ancient historians into a methodology and a standard, and above all to be able to draw upon the advantage of a far wider perspective. Classical historiography had confined itself to the stories of individual nations over a relatively short span of time, whereas the moderns were able to survey a wide range of different cultures, comparing and contrasting them, and to consider them all within the general heading of the entire historical development of mankind.

> The observer's eye may acquire a singular acuteness by the comparative study of as many nations as possible, especially of those which have already passed

away. Could anyone contemplate the history of mankind as a whole, of which the history of individual nations are but the parts, the successive steps in the evolution of humanity would of course afford him a similar objective rule for all these points in which whole peoples permanently differ from one another.[7]

In contradistinction to all historical theory deducing its findings from the past, we take as our actual, even necessary, starting-point that moment in history where the present spectator enjoys the inestimable advantage of observing the occurring events in the light of his own experience, and perceives, although chained to the rocks of time, the approach of Oceanus' daughters.[8]

For writers who did not consider themselves historians but drew on the historical perspective in their studies of economic and social development, modernity possessed a further advantage in being able to utilize an advanced understanding of the workings of society, which could then be applied to the past. It remained a matter of dispute, as exemplified in Marx's critique of political economy, how far modern terms might be used in studying past societies and how far past evidence could be considered relevant to present concerns in an entirely different form of society. John Stuart Mill exemplifies the view that the past could be of only limited use in the present:

There is not a fact in history which is not susceptible of as many different explanations as there are possible theories of human affairs. Not only is history not the source of political philosophy, but the profoundest political philosophy is requisite to explain history; without it all in history which is worth understanding remains mysterious . . . History is not the foundation, but the verification, of the social science; it corroborates, and often suggests, political truths, but cannot prove them. The proof of them is drawn from the laws of human nature, ascertained through the study of ourselves by reflection, and of mankind by actual intercourse with them. That what we know of former ages, like what we know of foreign nations, is, with all its imperfections, of much use, by correcting the narrowness incident to personal experience, is undeniable; but the usefulness of history depends upon its being kept in the second place.[9]

The growing sense of difference between past and present, so that the past could no longer serve as a source of examples or precepts relevant to present concerns, suggested that it might reasonably be ignored altogether by those concerned with the state of contemporary society.[10] The contrary argument was that the past was relevant precisely because it was different; the confrontation of ancient and modern was essential, partly in order to reveal the existence of universal principles of human behavior that transcended specific cultural contexts but above all to highlight the distinctive character of modernity and the nature of the development that explains the change from present to past.[11] In practice, however, the actual results of these investigations might offer further support for the rejection of history in favor of more present-oriented disciplines; not so much because it was felt to be irrelevant to the present as because its implications for the fate of modernity itself seemed to be so disturbing.

The Shape of History

The nineteenth century was the great era of studies, which today would generally labeled "grand narratives," dedicated to comprehending historical development in terms of the working-out of different principles, such as the development of productive powers, or rationalization, or specialization, within human society over time.[12] Such processes could be elevated into the defining theme of the entirety of world-historical development, as in the accounts of Hegel or Marx, or simply followed through as a single thread in a multi-faceted process. It was perhaps the greatest advantage that modern historians held over their ancient predecessors: the recognition not only that the world of human affairs was subject to dramatic transformations over time but also that it might be possible to discern the logic of this development.

Attempts at identifying such underlying principles did not necessarily involve the detailed study of the entirety of world history. On the contrary, there was a marked tendency to ignore certain periods as being of little interest; the later Roman Empire was regarded by most commentators as not classical or as the period of the decadence and decline of the classical, and hence – even after Jacob Burckhardt had sought to establish "late antiquity" as a historical epoch in its own right – it was frequently ignored.[13] There was an even stronger tendency to dismiss non-European history as timeless, unchanging, and of little interest compared with the central drama of the rise of European modernity. As Mill argued, "the true ancestors of the European nations are not those from whose blood they are sprung, but those from whom they derive the richest portion of their inheritance. The battle of Marathon, even as an event in English history, is of more importance than the battle of Hastings."[14] The supposedly global historical accounts of both Hegel and Marx had their focus fixed firmly on the progression from Greece and Rome to medieval Europe and modernity. Marx notoriously dismissed the "Asiatic mode of production" as stagnant and incapable of development, while Hegel explicitly argued that the non-classical past, even or especially those parts of it which appeared to have developed a high level of sophistication and civilization, could be excluded from consideration because it lacked the elements which he identified as essential for historical development:

> For the first time in the state, with the consciousness of laws, do distinct actions take place, and with them the clarity of a consciousness of those actions, which gives the capability and the need to preserve them. It strikes anyone who begins to become acquainted with the treasures of Indian literature that this land, so rich in the most profound spiritual outputs, has no history . . . In this land the original organisation of differentiation in society became ossified at once as a "natural" order in the form of castes, so that the laws do indeed deal with civil rights but make them dependent on the natural distinctions . . . As a result the element of ethics is banished from the splendour of Indian life and its kingdoms.[15]

> Chinese morality has, since the Europeans first became acquainted with it and with the writings of Confucius, achieved the highest praise and appreciative acknowledgement of its excellence from those who are familiar with Christian morality. Likewise there is acknowledgement of the sublimity with which Indian religion and poetry (to be precise, poetry of the higher sort) and especially philosophy express and demand the renunciation and sacrifice of the sensual. Yet both these nations lack, one must say entirely lack, the essential consciousness of the concept of freedom. To the Chinese their moral laws are like natural laws, appearing as positive commands, compulsory rights and duties or rules of courtesy towards one another. Freedom, through which the substantive determinations of reason first become moral conviction, is lacking.[16]

This was not the only way in which the story of world history might be told; in Max Weber's account of the rise of modernity, for example, one key question is why antiquity – like China or India – had failed to develop capitalism in the way that late medieval Europe had done. Weber drew parallels between the classical and the oriental city, and between classical and oriental society, in opposition to later European modernity.

However, in practice, for all his emphasis on global comparisons, it was in the ancient Mediterranean world that he detected the embryonic traces of capitalism as a development which was eventually stifled through the bureaucratization of the Later Roman Empire and the collapse of its economic base.[17] Antiquity was not, in Weber's view, the direct point of origin of modernity, but there is a strong sense that it could have been; in establishing, through the elaboration of different ideal types, the conditions which promoted the rise of capitalism and those which impeded it, he presented classical antiquity as a key part of the story of European development in the way that China and India clearly were not.

Such accounts could be intellectually satisfying, promising an understanding of human history as, at root, a coherent and comprehensible process; they could also be reassuring. In place of a view of history as the fulfillment of an inscrutable divine plan, readers were offered a full explanation of the goals of history and its ultimate destination. It was relatively easy to conclude from most such grand narratives that modernity was the culmination and fulfillment of a natural and progressive development. This was the conclusion drawn by many economic writers, in the light of obvious improvements in material power and the control of nature that were interpreted as the result of the full development of human capacities; humanity had now reached the stage at which it was both fully cognizant of the true sources of prosperity and happiness and blessed with the social structures that would support and develop them further. It might prove necessary at times to qualify this view, in the light of the failure of modern society as yet to meet expectations in every respect; as the more skeptical, historically minded economist Wilhelm Roscher commented, "I have, myself, no doubt, that up to the present time, mankind, as a whole, has, from the beginning of historical knowledge, always advanced. In individual cases, their movement has been interrupted by so many pauses, and even by so many occasional retrogressions, that great care must be taken not to infer superior excellence from mere subsequency."[18] Considered in the long term, however, from the trans-historical, global – or at least European – perspective, it was difficult not to see the triumph of modernity as a positive, upwards development.

> The experience of the past proves, in the most decisive manner, that the progressive march of civilisation follows a natural and unavoidable course, which flows from the law of human organisation and, in its turn, becomes the supreme law of all practical phenomena . . . All men who possess a

certain knowledge of the leading facts of history, be their historical views what they may, will agree in this, that the cultivated portion of the human race, considered as a whole, has made uninterrupted progress in civilisation from the most remote periods of history to our own day.[19]

However, the grand narratives of human development did not invariably promote such self-satisfaction and confidence. Those who were unimpressed by the condition of modern society or culture could well doubt whether the story should properly be described as one of progress. It could be figured instead as degeneration and decline from an ideal state of nature, as Rousseau did, or as a process which had stalled at its penultimate stage and needed to progress further. Even if the gains of modernity were acknowledged as real, there was a question as to whether they were sufficient to justify the suffering of earlier generations that had been required to bring them about.

What remains disconcerting about all this is firstly, that the earlier generations seem to perform their laborious tasks only for the sake of the later ones, so as to prepare for them a further stage from which they can raise still higher the structure intended by nature; and secondly, that only the later generations will in fact have the good fortune to inhabit the building on which a whole series of their forefathers (admittedly, without any conscious intention) had worked without themselves being able to share in the happiness they were preparing.[20]

Hegel, for all his insistence on the truth of his interpretation of history – which clearly implied that the ends ultimately justified the means – was well aware of the way that this sort of account of the past could become a source of despair as much as a source of unwarranted self-satisfaction:

One can, without rhetorical exaggeration, merely with the correct putting-together of misfortune, establish the most fearful image of that development which the most splendid nations and states as well as private virtues have experienced, and with this arouse feelings of the deepest, most desperate sadness, which no consoling outcome is sufficient to counterbalance and against which we can strengthen ourselves or try to escape it only by thinking: it turned out like that once; it is fate; nothing can change it now – and then, by returning out of the boredom which this reflection of sadness could produce in us, back into our feeling for life, the present of our aims and interests, in short, into selfishness, which stands on a peaceful shore and enjoys from a position of safety the distant spectacle of the confused mass of wreckage. But even as we look upon history as this slaughter-bench on which the happiness of peoples, the wisdom of states and the virtue of individuals are sacrificed, so the question also of necessity comes to mind, for whom or for what final purpose these innumerable victims were offered up . . . Out of this we have determined that the events which present that picture for our dark feelings and thoughtful reflections upon them are the field in which we see only the means for what we maintain is the substantive purpose, the absolute final purpose or, what is the same thing, the true result of world-history.[21]

Another anxiety aroused by these global perspectives on history related to the strong sense of determinism that seemed to permeate them. Narratives like those of Hegel or Marx rest on the assumption that history has a coherent shape or logic that is capable of being discerned by human reason; historical development amounts to much more than the unpredictable actions of individuals or the vagaries of chance and accident – and that implies, or could imply, that individual freedom of action was absent or unimportant. This issue had already been identified by Kant.

History is concerned with giving an account of these phenomena, no matter how deeply concealed their causes may be, and it allows us to hope that, if it examines the free exercise of the human will *on a large scale*, it will be able to discover a regular progression among freely willed actions. In the same way, we may hope that what strikes us in the actions of individuals as confused and fortuitous may be recognised, in the history of the entire species, as a steadily advancing but slow development of man's original capacities . . . Individual men and even entire nations little imagine that, while they are pursuing their own ends, each in his own way and often in opposition to others, they are unwittingly guided in their advance along a course intended by nature. They are unconsciously promoting an end which, even if they knew what it was, would scarcely arouse their interest.[22]

Hegel echoed this argument almost exactly, which in turn was adopted by Marx with the claim that he had simply shifted the perspective from heaven – the focus on reason and intellect – to earth.

In world history, the actions of men can result in something completely different from what they aim at and achieve and from what they directly know and intend; they work for their own interests, but something else is thereby brought about, which is contained within their actions but which was not in their consciousness or in their intention.[23]

The reassurance that history had a coherent shape and direction, and that its course was ultimately positive and necessary – the development of the human spirit, the expansion of human capacities – brought with it also the fear that it was a process far beyond human control. Any doubts, then, as to whether the consequences of historical development were wholly positive or its trajectory wholly favorable to humanity were generally accompanied by a sense of helplessness in the face of vast impersonal forces.

Prophecies and Nightmares

Whether modernity regarded the past as irrelevant to its concerns or as essential for its own self-understanding, it could not wholly ignore questions about the nature and trajectory of historical development with regard to its own future. Civilization might have triumphed, but was that a permanent situation? As Immanuel Kant remarked, "the course which the human race follows on the way to fulfilling its destiny seems to be subject to incessant interruptions, with a constant risk of reverting to the original barbarism."[24] The Austrian poet and playwright Stefan Zweig, looking back from the middle of the twentieth century, ironically characterized the historical viewpoint of the late nineteenth: "one looked back with contempt at earlier epochs with their wars, famines and revolts, as belonging to a time when humanity was still underdeveloped and insufficiently enlightened."[25] Publicly, one might say, such self-confidence in the continued success of modernity was the norm. However, much nineteenth-century literature exhibits a fear of the return of the past in different guises, with Gothic novels dominated by the threat of atavistic forces like evil aristocrats, monks, ghosts, the nightmares of modernity; the "uncanny," interpreted by Freud as the return of the repressed, is a recurring theme.[26] If, as Jeffrey Wolfreys has suggested, "haunting exists in a certain relation to the identity of modernity," then it suggests that the triumph of modernity over the feudal past was not felt to be wholly secure.[27] Moreover, even if a revival of medievalism could be excluded, there was no guarantee that modernity would necessarily continue in its current form; the example of classical antiquity, known through its ruins and remnants, was the clearest possible indication of the impermanence of all human creations.[28]

Some grand narratives of history sought to provide reassurance by identifying the future trajectory of development as a continuation or intensification of the present: the economists, for example, saw the prospect of continuing growth, new technology, and ever-expanding prosperity. Critics of modernity like Schiller and Marx, on the other hand, were happy to insist on its impermanence, and looked instead to the society that would replace it with justice and equality for all. The "laws of motion" of history identified in its progress so far, pointed the way forward; the question was whether, as in Hegel's account, one simply had to wait for the fulfillment of history's purpose, or whether, as Marx and other radicals tended to argue, it was incumbent on individuals to help the process along through their own actions.

However, an alternative tradition of historical interpretation offered a gloomier picture of modernity's prospects; the habit of understanding human history in biological terms, as Roscher did in response to critics who sought to dismiss "lower" forms of civilization: "Whoever is acquainted with the development of the plant, cannot fail to see in the seed the germ of its growth, and in its flower, the herald of decay."[29] If human society is figured as a plant – or as an organism, with the concomitant tendency to evoke metaphors of the childhood and maturity of social and political systems – then we can indeed see the connection between ourselves and earlier forms of society, but eventual decline and decay are built into our expectations for the future rather than simply being a possible outcome of the historical process.

David Hume had forcefully addressed such arguments in the debate about whether the population of antiquity was greater than that of modernity on account of the youthful vigor of the world in the former period:

> There is very little ground, either from reason or observation, to conclude the world eternal or incorruptible . . . It must therefore, as well as each individual form which it contains, have its infancy, youth, manhood and old age; and it is probably that, in all these variations, man, equally with every animal and vegetable, will partake. In the flourishing age of the world, it may be expected, that the human species should possess greater vigour both of mind and body, more prosperous health, higher spirits, longer life, and a stronger inclination and power of generation. But if the general system of things, and human society of course, have any such gradual revolutions, they are too slow to be discernible in that short period which is comprehended by history and tradition.[30]

The perspective shifted, however, when historians identified an "intermediate" form of life between the world and individual creatures; that is to say, they understood societies and cultures in biological terms, with a lifespan much longer than their inhabitants but clearly finite in comparison with the world as a whole. History then provided numerous examples of the birth, growth, and decline of societies and civilizations:

> If Sparta and Rome perished, what state can hope to last forever? If we want to form a lasting establishment, let us therefore not dream of making it eternal. To succeed one must not attempt the impossible, nor flatter oneself that the work of men can be endowed with a solidity human things do not allow for. The body politic, just like the body of a man, begins to die as soon as it is born and carries within it the causes of its destruction.[31]

Such a view of history, then, suggested that modernity could not endure for ever; could a more detailed study of the past reveal more precise information about its current position, its prospects, and the possibility of averting its downfall? Once again, classical antiquity was central to the debate, but this time the focus was on Rome; Nietzsche was alone in interpreting the "decadence" of modern society and culture through a comparison with ancient Greece. In Britain, the discussions tended to focus on finding or disputing parallels between the Roman and British Empires; their political institutions, their relations with conquered territories and peoples, and their likely fates.[32] Elsewhere in Europe, Rome was seen as the exemplary complex civilization; if modern European civilization was to have any hope for the future, it was necessary to understand Rome's fall and to analyze how far the situations were analogous. The optimistic economist denied the existence of any significant parallel:

> It has almost become the fashion to compare our present with the period of decline of the Greek and Roman republics. Frightful parallel, in which the greatest and most undoubted differences were frequently overlooked for smaller and certainly questionable similarities. Is not the abolition of slavery . . . something new and of great import from a moral and economic point of view? . . . The discovery of the whole earth soon to be completed, and its probable consequence, the civilization of all nations of any importance, must remove the danger to which all the civilized nations of antiquity eventually succumbed, namely, destruction by entirely barbarous hordes.[33]

Weber's 1896 account of the decline of ancient civilization, meanwhile, explicitly noted that it carried no direct lessons about the likely fate of modernity, given the fundamental differences in economic organization between the two cultures.

A storyteller can always count on heightened interest if his listeners believe that the story applies to their own lives too. Then he can end with a moral exhortation. My story, however, is not of that sort. There is little or nothing which ancient history can teach us about our own social problems. A proletarian of today and a slave of antiquity would have as little in common as do a European and a Chinese. Our problems and those of antiquity are entirely different. Therefore the story I tell has only historical interest. Yet it is one of the most absorbing man knows, for it describes the internal disintegration of an ancient civilisation.[34]

Weber's analysis begins by rejecting the wide range of different explanations for the fall of Rome put forward by historians, including military defeat, political change, despotism, and luxury, and then interprets it in terms of cultural decline. "This civilisation had been in eclipse for a long time . . . When, after one and a half centuries of decline, the Western Empire finally disappeared, barbarism had already conquered the Empire from within."[35] This was to be explained by Rome's failure to allow capitalism to develop fully, above all because of slavery, resulting in due course in a withdrawal from the market, the decline of the cities, and a reversion to rural society. Clearly modernity had developed in a different direction and to a much greater degree; however, the fact that Weber presented Rome's fall in terms of a reversion to a "natural" economy, as if this was the default position of human society, established a sense of civilization as something artificial and fragile. In his later work, his arguments about the effects of bureaucratization and rationalization on Roman and modern society make the parallels seem rather closer.

   In the aftermath of the First World War, the critiques of modernity found in Marx, Nietzsche, and Weber's historical interpretations were incorporated into far more pessimistic readings. Oswald Spengler's account of the *Decline of the West* insisted on taking the organic metaphor entirely literally – "each culture has its own new possibilities of expression, which appear, ripen, decay and never return"[36] – and so presented western civilization as a strictly limited phenomenon whose fate was predetermined and clearly discernible in its historical predecessors.[37] The ancient historian M. I. Rostovtzeff, meanwhile, drew heavily on his own experiences of the Russian Revolution in his account of the end of the Roman Empire:

The evolution of the ancient world has a lesson and a warning for us. Our civilization will not last unless it be a civilization not of one class but of the masses . . . But the ultimate problem remains like a ghost, ever present and unlaid: Is it possible to extend a higher civilization to the lower classes without debasing its standards and diluting its quality to the vanishing point? Is not every civilization bound to decay as soon as it begins to penetrate the masses?[38]

The Weight of the Past

The implications of coherent, deterministic theories of history could create problems as much for those who wished to see the replacement of modernity by a better form of society as for those who sought its preservation. It was clearly necessary for radicals to insist on the possibility of continuing change, rather than accepting that modernity was the culmination of historical development and would now be succeeded by an endless, unchanging present. Marx, for example, sought to create space for an alternative narrative, in which the present was not the goal of history but its penultimate stage, and the decay of capitalism was precisely the moment when the future came within reach. His main weapon was critique of the sort of historical perspective that tried to discount any possibility of escaping the conditions of the present. As Hegel had noted, "even the common and average history-writer, who thinks and claims that he is merely receptive, devoting himself only to what is given, is not passive in his thought and brings along his own categories and sees everything through them."[39] Marx applied this insight to the accounts of political economists and historians, highlighting the way that their accounts sought to promote conservative political goals by presenting the particular conditions of modernity as the universal, unalterable condition of humanity. As he caustically summarized their approach, "thus there has been history, but there is no longer any."[40]

However, the importance of the past is not confined to its use in legitimizing and defending the present state of affairs. It plays a central role in influencing the ideas and hence the actions of individuals, so that understanding it is vital if there is to be any hope of persuading people to embrace the possibility of revolutionary change:

Men make their own history, but they do not make it just of their own free will; not under circumstances chosen by themselves, but under circumstances directly encountered, given and handed down. The tradition of all the dead generations weighs like a nightmare on the brains of the living. And if they nevertheless seem engaged in revolutionising themselves and things, in creating something that has not yet existed, precisely in such periods of revolutionary crisis they fearfully conjure up the spirits of the past to their service, borrow from them names, battle cries and costumes, in order to present the new scene of world-history in this time-honoured clothing and with this borrowed language. Thus Luther masked himself as the Apostle Paul, the Revolution of 1789 to 1814 draped itself alternately as the Roman republic and the Roman empire, and the Revolution of 1848 knew nothing better than to parody, now 1789, now the revolutionary tradition of 1793–5.[41]

This passage is commonly cited as an example of Marxian irony – it begins with his famous remark about events in world history occurring twice, "the first time as tragedy, the second as farce" – or in discussions of the nature of determinism and the role of human agency in history. It is most interesting in the present context as an analysis of why people need history, and the implications of this for the way that the classical past was used and reinterpreted within modernity. The recourse to ancient examples is recognized by Marx as potentially liberating, above all in a society which values (or overvalues) tradition as the basis for the organization of society. The past, or more usually certain specific aspects of the past, become a source of inspiration to action, a source of costumes and phrases, a means of legitimizing revolutionary change by presenting it as a return to the past and a restoration. The revolution in this case was in the cause of the unheroic goal of establishing the rule of the bourgeoisie over society, scarcely something (in Marx's view) to inspire heroism and sacrifice on its behalf, but,

> in the classically austere traditions of the Roman republic, its gladiators found the ideals and the art forms, the self-deceptions that they needed in order to conceal from themselves the bourgeois limitations of the content of their struggles and to keep their enthusiasm on the high plane of the great historical tragedy . . . Thus the awakening of the dead in those revolutions served the purpose of glorifying the new struggles, not of parodying the old; of magnifying the given task in imagination, not of fleeing from its solution in reality; of finding once more the spirit of revolution, not of making its ghost walk again.[42]

One important conclusion from this is that history shows that revolution was once both possible and desirable; identification with the past enables the belief that the emulation of the past is also possible and desirable. People need to learn a new language for a new society, initially by translating everything back into the familiar language of classical liberty and heroism; this then becomes fully assimilated and the old language is forgotten. However, now that bourgeois society has been achieved, the past has ceased to have the same power. The *bourgeois* monarch Louis Bonaparte produces only a parody of a true revolution, while the true revolutionaries now need to free themselves from precedent:

> The social revolution of the nineteenth century cannot draw its poetry from the past, but only from the future. It cannot begin with itself before it has cast off every superstition about the past. The earlier revolutions required world-historical memories in order to anaesthetise themselves concerning their own content. The revolution of the nineteenth century must let the dead bury their dead, in order to arrive at its own content.[43]

It has become possible, Marx argues, to cast aside history, as there is no need to conceal the true implications of modern revolution – it *is* heroic and in the interests of justice, rather than simply claiming to be so. However, it has also become *necessary* to cast aside the past; the constant danger is that revolutionary action might seem to be doomed, to betray its ideals if not to fail altogether, if it is seen only through the eyes of historical precedent. History – or at least certain versions of history – establishes a belief in an eternal and universal human nature that appears antithetical to a society based on equality and community rather than self-interest and competition. Too much faith in what can be learnt from history is ultimately an impediment to change, even if it can also be a spur to action.

There are some significant parallels between Marx's critique of the uses of the past and the more extensive investigation of the psychological roots of historical knowledge developed by Nietzsche, above all in his second *Untimely Meditation* on "The uses and disadvantages of history for life." History, Nietzsche suggests, has the power to undermine the claims of modernity and to reveal that society is susceptible to change; it reveals the origins of things that might otherwise appear eternal and immovable:

> Education is first lessons in what is necessary, then in what is changing and inconstant. One leads the youth into nature, and shows him everywhere the rule of laws; then the laws of bourgeois society. Here already the question will arise: *must* this be so? Gradually he needs history, in order to hear how this has come to be. But thereby he learns that it can also be different. How much power does man have over things? This is the question in all

education. In order now to show how things can be completely different, one points for example to the Greeks. One needs the Romans to show how they became as they are.[44]

However, all too often historical study serves in practice to frustrate any desire for change, by presenting the present as the natural and inevitable outcome of historical development. The "monumental" history that represents the past as a succession of great moments and immortal human achievements, of which the present is the triumphant culmination, "deceives through analogies": "How much difference must be overlooked, if it is to have that powerful effect, how violently must the individuality of the past be squeezed into a general form, and all its sharp corners and outlines broken off for the sake of conformity"; "it will always have to approximate, generalise and make the dissimilar similar, it will always have to tone down differences in motives and causes."[45] The study of the past "for its own sake," meanwhile, the antiquarian habit of preservation and reverence, offers comfort and reassurance, a sense of continuity and stability; however, it "no longer conserves life but mummifies it," undermining any belief in or desire for the possibility of change: "in the end everything old and past that enters the field of vision at all is simply taken to be equally worthy of respect, but everything that approaches this antiquity without reverence, everything new and changing, is rejected and treated as an enemy."[46]

> Antiquarian history itself degenerates from the moment it is no longer animated and inspired by the fresh life of the present. Its piety dries up, the scholarly habit continues without it and revolves with egoistic self-satisfaction around its own axis. Then one sees the horrible spectacle of a blind fury for collecting, a restless scrabbling together of everything that has ever existed. Man wraps himself up in mustiness.[47]

Even "critical" history, the condemnation and rejection of the past in the interests of the present and the future – not least in the face of the antiquarian demand that everything which has grown old should be made immortal – is based on a dangerous self-deception and denial, the illusion of superiority:

> Because we are the product of earlier generations, we are also the product of their aberrations, passions and errors, and their crimes; it is not possible to free oneself completely from this chain. If we condemn these

aberrations and consider ourselves as free from them, this does not do away with the fact that we come from them.[48]

In other words, each and any historical account needs to be interrogated about the needs and desires which it serves. It is easy, then, to see how belief in historical progress and in the triumph of modernity is a self-serving illusion worthy only of mockery:

> Consideration of history has never flown so far before, not even in its dreams; for now the history of men is only the latest instalment of the history of animals and plants; even in the lowest depths of the sea the universal historian still finds the traces of himself, as living slime; marvelling, as if at a miracle, at the immense distance which mankind has already covered, his vision is overcome by vertigo before the still more astonishing miracle, modern man himself, who is able to comprehend his own development. He stands high and proud on the pyramid of the world-process; as he sets the keystone of his knowledge upon it, he seems to call out to nature listening around him, "We are at the goal, we are the goal, we are the completion of nature."
>
> Over-proud European of the nineteenth century, you are raving! Your knowledge does not complete nature, but only kills your own nature. Simply measure your heights as a knower against your depths as a doer. Certainly you climb on the sunbeams of knowledge towards heaven, but also downwards towards chaos. Your manner of proceeding, as a climber upon knowledge, is your undoing; the solid earth gives way into uncertainty; there is no longer any support for your life, only spiders' threads, which each new grab for knowledge tears apart.[49]

In Marx's analysis, the evocation of the past as a basis for present action by Luther and the French revolutionaries is contrasted with the apparently spontaneous and wholly authentic actions of their classical models. Nietzsche makes this contrast still more explicit. All humans need history, he argues, if they are to distinguish themselves from the animals that live only in the present, and it is a universal condition that "man braces himself against the great and ever greater weight of the past; this presses him down or pushes him sideways, it impedes his progress as a dark and invisible burden."[50] We would not be human without the capacity to remember – but it is equally necessary to be able to forget: "the unhistorical and the historical are necessary in equal measure for the health of an individual, of a people and of a culture."[51] An overwhelming concern with history is something distinctive to modernity; it can feel rightly proud of its development of the subject, but it also runs the risk of serious injury as a result. The modern historical sense epitomizes modernity's cultural problems: the accumulation of knowledge as an end in itself, the gathering together of countless past cultures as if this constituted culture, the lack of anything of its own. The oversaturation of an age with history is hostile and dangerous to life, leading to stagnation or despair:

> Through this excess a period develops the conceit that it possesses the rarest virtue, justice, to a higher degree than any other age; through this excess the instincts of a people are disturbed and the individual no less than the whole is hindered in development; through this excess the belief, harmful at any time, in the old age of mankind, the belief that one is a latecomer and an epigone, is implanted; through this excess a period comes into the dangerous mood of irony about itself and from this into the still more dangerous mood of cynicism.[52]

Just as Marx feared that the historical sense would persuade people that there is no realistic prospect of a better form of society, and would thus undermine any attempt at creating one, so Nietzsche's concern is that it will destroy any belief in the possibility of overcoming the limits of modern society and culture. "The historical sense, if it rules *without restraint* and realises all its consequences, uproots the future, because it destroys illusions and robs the things that exist of the atmosphere in which alone they can live."[53] Nietzsche emphasizes the necessity of identifying "the boundary at which the past must be forgotten if it is not to become the gravedigger of the present,"[54] and offers an argument very similar to that of Marx about the use of the costumes and phrases of the past as an inspiration:

> The man who no longer dares to trust himself but involuntarily asks history for advice on his feelings – "How should I feel about this?" – gradually becomes through his timidity an actor, and plays a role, more often a number of roles, and therefore plays them badly and shallowly. Gradually all congruence between the man and his historical context is lost; we see impertinent little fellows associating with the Romans as if they were people just like them, and they scrabble and dig in the remains of Greek poets as if these *corpora* had been provided for their dissection and were as *vilia* as their own literary *corpora* may be.[55]

Overcoming History

> The dangerous meaning of *art*: as the custodian and galvanizer of dead and dying conceptions. *History*, in so far as it wishes to push us back into feelings which we have overcome. To feel "historically," "to be just towards the past," is only possible if we are already well beyond it. But the danger in the feeling required for this is great: let us leave the dead to bury their dead, so that we do not take on the stench of corpses.
>
> F. Nietzsche, *Wir Philologen*, 160

How is modernity to overcome the pernicious influence of the past? Marx attempted to do so by means of a historical critique, questioning the underlying assumptions of existing accounts of human development and demonstrating, historically, that alternatives to the present state of affairs are possible. The contradictions in this approach are obvious. Marx's account is just as inspired by his own economic and political assumptions as are those of his opponents, and his ideological critique of their self-serving narratives could easily be turned on his own version of the past. Moreover, his call for the abandonment of the past as the basis for action sits oddly with his own practices: his regular citation of classical examples and precedents, his desire to see classical culture somehow revived and recreated within the society that is to come, and his constant emphasis on the historical perspective as the key to understanding the present. It is as if the *Eighteenth Brumaire* is, unknowingly, a piece of self-analysis as much as an examination of the tendency of others to lean on the past as a crutch.

Nietzsche's approach is more subtle, but equally problematic. He recognizes the indispensability of the historical sense as part of what it is to be human; what is required is the right sort of historical sense, kept in equal balance with the unhistorical, above all by keeping in mind the idea that history must serve a higher purpose rather than being an end in itself. "Our estimation of the historical may be only an occidental prejudice; let us at least make some progress with this prejudice and not stand still! Let us only learn ever better how to employ history for the purpose of *life*!"[56] Each of the three forms of history which he has identified can have positive attributes in this respect. From the monumental approach, the historian "takes from it that the greatness that once existed was once *possible* and therefore may once again be possible."[57] The antiquarian preserves for future generations the past, and looks beyond his own existence to the spirit of his house, his city, and his race; he greets the soul of his nation across the long dark centuries of confusion as his own soul, and gives people a sense of belonging within the confines of their own culture. The critical historian, meanwhile, creates a space for the future to come into being by breaking up and dissolving parts of the past. There are then the historical men, those who continue to believe that there is value both in existence and in the past.

> We will call them the historical men: looking into the past drives them towards the future, fires up their courage to continue to hold on to life and kindles that justice will still be done and that happiness lies behind the hill towards which they are advancing. These historical men believe that the meaning of existence will come more and more to light in the course of its *process*, they look backwards only so that, through consideration of the process so far, they can learn to understand the present and to desire the future more fiercely; they have no idea how unhistorically they think and act, despite all their history, nor how their preoccupation with history stands in the service, not of pure knowledge, but of life.[58]

Nietzsche returns again and again to the theme of the necessity of boundaries and illusions; somehow, one must know not to know too much. The weight of past precedent, above all the awful example of the Greeks, could always be a source of despair at modernity's inability to emulate or surpass the achievements of its predecessors; but, with the correct attitude, this did not have to be the case.

> Even if we Germans were nothing but successors – we could, if we looked on such an image as an inheritance dedicated to us, never be anything greater or prouder than successors. What I mean by this, and nothing else, is that the often painful thought of being an epigone can guarantee great effects and a desire for the future rich with hope, for an individual as much as for a people: if we understand ourselves as the heirs and successors of classical and astonishing powers and see in this our honour and our spur. Not like faded and wasted remnants of a strong race, who eke out a frosty existence as antiquarians and grave-diggers of that race. Such latelings certainly live an ironic existence; annihilation follows at the heels of their limping life's-course; they shudder, if they rejoice at the past, because they are living memories and yet their memory is senseless without heirs.[59]

Nietzsche has no time for the triumphalism of the Hegelian belief that the present is the zenith of human achievement; such an attitude is fatal.

"Certainly it is a paralysing and upsetting belief that one is a late descendant of the ages; but it must appear terrifying and destructive if such a belief one day with a bold reversal raises the lateling to divinity as the true meaning and goal of all previous events, if his self-conscious misery is equated with a fulfilment of World History."[60] Rather, he insists on the need for further change, for the creation of a new generation, inoculated with the unhistorical and the suprahistorical, with the power to forget as well as to remember. "It is probable that we, the historically-sick, will also have to suffer from the antidotes. But that we suffer from them is no proof against the correctness of the chosen treatment."[61]

Is such a renewal conceivable? Nietzsche turns, as he says, from the doubters to the company of the hopeful, "in order to narrate to them through a parable the course and progress of their cure, their delivery from the historical sickness, and thereby their own history, up to the point where they will be sufficiently healthy again to pursue history."[62] The message is that of the god of Delphi: know thyself.

There were centuries in which the Greeks found themselves in a danger similar to that in which we find ourselves, namely that of being overwhelmed by the other and the past, of perishing through "history." They never lived in proud inviolability: their "culture" was rather for a long time a chaos of foreign, Semitic, Babylonian, Lydian, Egyptian forms and ideas . . . And nevertheless Hellenic culture was no aggregate, thanks to that Apollonian oracle. The Greeks gradually learned to *organize the chaos*, because, following the Delphic teaching, they thought back to themselves, that is to say to their real needs, and let the pseudo-needs die out. So they again took possession of themselves; they did not long remain the overburdened heirs and epigones of the entire Orient; they became, after exhausting struggle with themselves, through the practical interpretation of that oracle, the happiest enrichers and augmenters of the inherited treasure and the first-born and model of all future cultured peoples.[63]

Those who create a new culture, however dependent on their inheritance from others, will cease to be epigones; the second nature, chosen and learned, becomes a first nature – rather as Marx had suggested that it was possible to assimilate the language and ideals of the past and make them into one's own. The turn to the Greeks in this spirit will then reveal the meaning of true culture, in antithesis to the "merely decorative" culture or cultivatedness held in esteem in the modern world.

The paradox is obvious, and surely deliberate: Nietzsche's readers are to be reassured about the possibility of attaining a new culture and over-coming the pernicious influence of an excess of history by means of an account of the past that has to be read in the light of the foregoing critique of all historical narratives as self-serving and mythologizing – and potentially also in the light of his critique of "classicism" as the mythology of modernity.[64] Nietzsche's narrative is as naively "optimistic" an interpretation of the workings of history as any belief in scientific and economic progress or the triumph of bourgeois morality. Like Marx's approach to confronting the "nightmare" of history, its credibility depends ultimately on the reader's willingness, on the basis of agreement with the writer's political or moral agenda, to accept it as an account that somehow transcends the problems inherent in any other version of the past. However, Marx's account at least claims to be replacing the mythologies and illusions of the past with scientific truth, and so presents itself as something that could legitimately form the basis for individual action in the modern world. Nietzsche is entirely candid about the fact that he is seeking to put forward a new myth, which will fulfill the same function as earlier mythologies of giving meaning to life and so energizing individuals to break free of the tyranny of the past. The question, which Nietzsche's account leaves entirely open, is whether a myth can serve that purpose if it is known to be a myth, and whether the example of the Greeks can produce inspiration even when it has already been revealed as a modern illusion.

Notes

1 *Vorlesungen über die Philosophie der Geschichte*, 11–29. See Houlgate (1991); McCarney (2000).
2 See Momigliano (1990) and the essays collected in Nippel (1993).
3 Cf. Luce and Woodman (1993).
4 Meinecke (1972); Reill (1975); Krieger (1977).
5 Cf. Geuss (2005).
6 *Götzen-Dämmerung*, 156.
7 Roscher, *Principles of Political Economy*, I, 114–15.
8 Tönnies, *Community and Society*, 235; the end of the passage is a reference to Aeschylus' *Prometheus*, line 115.
9 Mill, "Sedgwick's Discourse," 44–5.
10 Koselleck (2004), 26–42.

11 Generally on the theme of "historicism," Meinecke (1972); Reill (1975); Hamilton (1996).
12 Generally, Callinicos (1995).
13 Cf. Brown (1971).
14 "Grote's History of Greece I," 273.
15 *Vorlesungen über die Philosophie der Geschichte*, 84.
16 Ibid., 95–6.
17 "Social causes," *passim*; *Agrarian Sociology of Ancient Civilizations*, 365–6.
18 Roscher, *Principles of Political Economy*, I, 143 note.
19 Comte, "Plan of the scientific operations," 143.
20 Kant, "Universal history," 44.
21 Hegel, *Vorlesungen über die Philosophie der Geschichte*, 35.
22 Kant, "Universal history," 41.
23 Hegel, *Vorlesungen über die Philosophie der Geschichte*, 42–3.
24 Kant, "Conjectures on the beginning of human history," 228 note.
25 Zweig, *Die Welt von Gestern*, 15.
26 Punter (1980).
27 Wolfreys (2001), 2. Cf. Derrida (1994).
28 Edwards (1999), especially the papers by Kennedy, Chard, and Martindale.
29 *Principles of Political Economy*, I, 113.
30 "On the populousness of antient nations," 381–2.
31 Rousseau, *Social Contract*, III.11.1–2.
32 Edwards (1999), esp. papers by Marjeed and Edwards; Hingley (2000).
33 Roscher, *Principles of Political Economy*, II, 388–9.
34 "Social causes," 390–1.
35 Ibid., 389.
36 *Der Untergang des Abendlandes*, 29.
37 Morley (2004b).
38 Rostovtzeff, (1926), 541.
39 Hegel, *Vorlesungen über die Philosophie der Geschichte*, 23.
40 *Poverty of Philosophy*, 121.
41 Marx, *Die achtzehnte Brumaire*, 115.
42 Ibid., 116.
43 Ibid., 117.
44 *Wir Philologen*, 135.
45 Nietzsche, *Vom Nutzen und Nachtheil der Historie*, 261–2.
46 Ibid., 267–8.
47 Ibid., 268.
48 Ibid., 270.
49 Ibid., 312–13.
50 Ibid., 249.
51 Ibid., 252.

52   Ibid., 279.
53   Ibid., 295.
54   Ibid., 251.
55   Ibid., 283.
56   Ibid., 256–7.
57   Ibid., 260.
58   Ibid., 255.
59   Ibid., 306–7.
60   Ibid., 308.
61   Ibid., 331.
62   Ibid., 332.
63   Ibid., 333.
64   Cf. Morley (2004c).

6

Allusion and Appropriation

The Rhetorical Uses of Antiquity

Looking into the matter more closely, it is difficult to decide who was the greater hypocrite: Louis XIV, when he sat and heard the Grecian hatred of tyrants declaimed in polished verses from the boards of his court theatre, or Corneille and Racine, when, to win the favour of their lord, they set in the mouths of their stage-heroes the warm words of freedom and political virtue of ancient Greece and Rome.

R. Wagner, *Art and Revolution*, 41

What is a legitimate use, or an acceptable appropriation, of antiquity? Wagner argues here that the original democratic context of Greek tragedy ought to determine, or at least set limits on, the range of possible interpretations; the dramas of classical Athens, even when they deal with the actions of kings and rulers, ought not to be capable of being made acceptable to a modern monarch. From the point of view of modern reception studies, such outrage misses the point; what interests us is the way that texts are reinterpreted and reimagined for new historical situations, rather than insisting on the existence of a single, objectively verifiable meaning.[1] The same can be said for the reception of the idea of antiquity, the set of images, associations, and "facts" concerning classical Greece and Rome that is transmitted, transmuted, and endlessly debated through modern European history.

However, part of the history of this reception is the history of disputes over the use and abuse of antiquity, the assertion of claims of ownership and the dismissal of the claims of others. Further, when the avowed intention is to apply an interpretation of antiquity to the understanding of the modern world and to plans for future action, there seems to be a greater need to engage with the question of what limits, if any, might be set to the appropriation of the classical, and what criteria might be called upon to evaluate it. Studies of the twentieth-century fascist use of classical culture can disavow the use of terms like "misappropriation" and "abuse" in the cause of gaining a true understanding of the dynamics of appropriation, in part because they can rely on the existence of an unspoken consensus, at least within academia, that the agenda of fascism was indisputably wrong.[2] In considering the radically different readings of antiquity offered by, say, Marx and Nietzsche, in support of radically different political agendas, the vocabulary of "abuse" and "misappropriation" can seem more necessary precisely because there is no such universal agreement on the validity or morality of their prescriptions for the modern world.

Within nineteenth-century debates, the vast majority of writers asserted the credibility of their accounts of antiquity on the basis of claims to factual accuracy and fidelity to the past, and disparaged the accounts of their opponents on philological or historical grounds. They took it for granted that history is both knowable and, for the most part, known; the possibility exists, if a correct methodology is chosen, of establishing an objective account of the past with which modern society can be compared and against which it can be evaluated. Nietzsche represents a partial exception to this approach since, at least some of the time, he is engaged on a different project, that of exposing the problematic and self-serving nature of all accounts of antiquity through a mixture of hyperbolic classicism, deliberate inconsistency, and explicit disregard for the norms of philological argument.[3] Nietzsche's project in fact highlights the problem in evaluating any of these different accounts of antiquity; they are all, in different ways, self-serving, and their claims of objectivity and accuracy can always be questioned on either political or psychological grounds.

We are faced with multiple versions of antiquity because of the existence of multiple interpretations of the nature of society; it was always possible to interpret the remains of antiquity differently, just as there was – until one chose to adopt the perspective of one or other of the competing accounts – no final or definitive understanding of modernity. Philological arguments were and are never final; "antiquity" was and is not a stable, known object that can be compared with a stable, known present. Historical evidence and methodology can exclude some interpretations of the past as manifestly implausible, even in the context of nineteenth-century knowledge and understanding of antiquity, but the majority of interpretations are at least defensible, not wholly incompatible with the surviving evidence. They cannot be labeled as abuses or misappropriations simply on the basis that they no longer conform to our understanding of ancient society.

If historical and empirical arguments are inadequate to differentiate between the multiplicity of interpretations and uses of the past, we are left with three possible approaches: those taken by Marx, Hegel, and Nietzsche respectively. Marx presents his own account of the past as objectively true, in contrast to the ideologically distorted accounts of those who see, for example, capitalism as a universal trait of human nature, but he also argues that all descriptions of the world are inevitably subjective, developed from within an already-existing set of assumptions, preconceptions, and values. Any given use of antiquity needs to be understood within this context, as Marx aims to critique political economy using its own categories of thought, but ultimately our judgment between different versions must rest on our own assumptions and values. Writers such as Rousseau, Schiller, or Mill present an antiquity that is consistent with their broader views of society and culture, if not wholly subordinate to them, and so vulnerable to the same criticisms that might be leveled against their overall philosophical frameworks. Value judgments on personal political grounds, even if these are disguised as empirical arguments, are ultimately unavoidable; there is no neutral, non-political, disinterested account of either present or past.

Hegel also explored the limits of empiricism, identifying the potential for conflict between history, in which "our thinking is subordinate to the given and to what exists," and philosophy, which develops ideas on the basis of speculation from within itself. "We must not let ourselves be led astray by the professional historians, because they, especially the Germans, who possess great authority, do exactly what they accuse philosophers of doing, namely creating *a priori* fabrications in history."[4] Even the ordinary historian naturally approaches the past with a preconceived set of categories, and interprets the data through them. From a philosophical point of view historians' categories tend to be inadequately defined or developed; however, consideration of the past on the basis of an assumption of its intelligibility – "the firm and unconquerable belief that there is reason in history" – will, in Hegel's view, produce a true understanding of the course of its development. The proper criterion for evaluating an account of the past or the deployment of antiquity in the consideration of modernity – bearing in mind that "when we go over the past, we are really concerned only with the present. This is because philosophy, which

occupies itself with the true, is concerned with what is eternally present"
– is the philosophical coherence of the categories of analysis:

> Such ideas then appear as something alien, external to the subject-matter.
> To the subjective culture, which does not have close acquaintance or
> familiarity with pure thought, they are indeed alien, and are not part of the
> conception or understanding of the subject matter which results from such
> a lack of familiarity. From this follows the statement that philosophy does
> not understand this sort of science. Philosophy must in fact admit that it
> does not have the understanding that dominates in such sciences and does
> not proceed according to the categories of that understanding, but rather
> according to the categories of reason, whereby it knows the value and
> status of that understanding.[5]

Objectivity is now located not in an empirically established past but in
philosophically established categories through which the past becomes intel-
ligible. From outside the Hegelian system, of course, this appears simply
as the assumption that interpretations of antiquity are to be judged valid
insofar as they are compatible with Hegelian philosophy – but also that
they might be evaluated in terms of their success in leading the reader
to adopt this perspective.

> The screen best suited to perform this task of estrangement for the sake of
> education is the world and language of the ancients. This world separates
> us from ourselves, but at the same time it grants us the cardinal means
> of returning to ourselves: we reconcile ourselves with it and thereby find
> ourselves again in it; but the self which we then find is the one which accords
> with the tone and universal essence of mind.[6]

This resembles, to some extent, Nietzsche's approach. All accounts
of the past in his view are to a greater or lesser extent self-serving,
delusional, and illusory, driven solely by the unacknowledged desires and
emotions of their creators; they reveal nothing about the past, but only
about the present. If this perspective is accepted, then the only criterion
for the evaluation of these accounts must be their impact on the present
in the service of Life, their success in creating alienation and dissatisfaction and in engendering "total enmity between our present 'culture' and
antiquity" – in other words, their success in converting the reader to
the Nietzschean perspective.[7] This constitutes the basis for Nietzsche's
scathing dismissal of virtually all contemporary classical studies:

The relation of the philologist to antiquity is *apologetic*, or inspired by the intention of detecting the things that our age respects in antiquity. The correct starting-point is the reverse: namely to start from an insight into modern topsy-turviness and to look back from antiquity to it – much that is very offensive in antiquity appears then as the most profound necessity.[8]

Precisely in those circles whose dignity could be to draw inexhaustibly from the Greek river to the benefit of German culture, in the circles of the university teachers, one has learnt best to come to terms with the Greeks promptly and in a comfortable manner, all too often to the extent of a sceptical abandonment of the Hellenic ideal and a complete reversal of the true purpose of all study of antiquity.[9]

Were we trained in a single one of the antique virtues and in the manner in which the ancients practised it? Was all reflection on morality not utterly lacking in our education – not to speak of the only possible critique of morality, a brave and rigorous attempt to live in this or that morality? Was there ever aroused in us any feeling that the ancients regarded more highly than the moderns? Were we ever shown the divisions of the day and of life, and goals beyond life, in the spirit of antiquity? Did we learn even the ancient languages in the way we learn those of living nations – namely, so as to speak them with ease and fluency? Not one real piece of ability, of new capacity, out of years of effort. Only a knowledge of what men were once capable of knowing.[10]

For Nietzsche, the philologist is the archetypal modern, exemplifying in his misappropriation and abuse of the classical past the deficiencies and sickness of modern culture. An account of antiquity, like an account of modernity, can in the end be judged only on the basis of its intentions and effects; for Nietzsche, on the basis of whether it seeks to make the classical world complicit with the present, or uses it to inspire dissatisfaction and discontent.

Allusions and Arguments

Leaving aside the question of whether this takes us any further in choosing between different versions of the past, each of which would see "the true purpose of the study of antiquity" in quite different terms, these three perspectives emphasize the different ways in which antiquity might be used;

it may be invoked not simply or necessarily as a means of developing substantive arguments so much as a means of provoking or inspiring a particular reaction in the reader, whether a complacent acceptance of modernity or a fierce dissatisfaction with it. The turn to the past as a means of understanding the present was based on well-founded and widely accepted arguments about the necessity of understanding objects through the study of their origins and development; but that does not exclude the possibility that a historically based account could also thereby draw upon the widespread respect and reverence for the past, especially the classical past, for rhetorical purposes. As the economic historian W. J. Ashley observed, "It is very noticeable to anyone who has come into contact with popular socialistic or revolutionary movements that an alleged historical fact has often more hold upon men's minds than any theoretic argument."[11] The rhetorical impact of a classical reference or historical example could be quite as important in making an account plausible as the content of the substantive arguments which, supposedly, such references and examples were intended to decorate or support.

Eighteenth- and nineteenth-century accounts of modernity are littered with classical allusions, examples, and references. The question is how they should be evaluated, and how one might – in the absence of a clear signal of intent – distinguish between the different purposes for which such allusions might be deployed. In any given instance, the introduction of a classical reference might be a deliberate move in the argument, or an incidental revelation of the writer's underlying assumptions about the relation between past and present and the relevance of history; it might be an unconscious reflection of their educational background in the classics, such that a classical allusion was simply a natural recourse, or a deliberate rhetorical tactic, drawing upon the reservoir of respect and reverence for classical antiquity. The one thing it is unlikely to be is wholly accidental and insignificant. Classicism may have pervaded eighteenth- and nineteenth-century culture, but in the analysis of social or economic structures allusions to classical antiquity were not ubiquitous; they must reflect the intellectual baggage of a particular writer, where they are not a deliberate choice.

For example, we might consider Marx's use of Aristotle, indisputably an important influence on his ideas and on *Kapital* in particular.[12] The structure of that work can be seen as a deliberate echoing of Aristotle's approach to philosophical analysis, and he is cited directly on a succession of key points, characterized as "a giant thinker" and "the greatest thinker of antiquity."[13] It is entirely possible to read these passages as constituting a sustained argument, in which Marx aims to build an ethical and social theory of political economy on Aristotelian lines. However, this is not the whole story. It is important to note that Aristotle is just as often cited as an example of error or of a limited, inadequate perspective as he is quoted as an authority. On the one hand he is claimed as a predecessor in identifying an issue that needed to be addressed but was taken for granted by modern economics; Marx's choice of approach, seeking to analyze the nature and origins of exchange value, is validated as having universal significance by the fact that it was identified as a vital problem by the key philosopher of antiquity. On the other hand it is made equally clear that Marx has surpassed his predecessor, and indeed for Marx to be correct Aristotle has to be shown to be wrong, or at least limited in his perspective:

> The genius of Aristotle shines out precisely in his discovery of a relation of equality in the value-expression of commodities. Only the historical barrier of the society in which he lived prevented him from finding out what "in reality" this relation of equality consisted of.[14]

Rather like Marx's analysis of classical culture, which he shows to be simultaneously limited and unsurpassable, past and present, but which serves above all as the basis for the critique of the inadequacies of the present, so the main purpose of the citation of Aristotle is to expose the limitations of contemporary economic thought. It seems fair to describe Marx as appropriating Aristotle for his own purposes: not his ideas, but his image, the place which he held in modern thought and culture.

It is clear that Marx engaged with Aristotle's thought over a long period, even if the relationship needs to be understood in more complex terms than simply one of "influence." The same can be said of his doctoral studies on the presocratic philosophers, which were bound up with his adoption and development of Hegelian ideas.[15] It is more difficult to know how to interpret the many other references to classical texts and examples throughout his writings. Marx calls on a common store of classical references, both inserting himself into that cultural tradition and using it as a means of criticizing or abusing other writers: one of his opponents is described as "the Pindar of the automatic factory," while "the Liverpool 'quality' have remained the Pindars of the slave trade."[16] Classical literature represents a source of powerful images, or at least images that are powerful to those with a similar background in the classics. The effect can be impressive, but runs the risk of incongruity or hyperbole: "the law which always holds the relative overpopulation or industrial reserve army in equilibrium with the extent and energy of accumulation rivets the worker to capital more firmly than the wedges of Hephaestus held Prometheus to the rock."[17] Marx had previously offered the more familiar identification of Prometheus with critical philosophy – "The declaration of Prometheus – 'In one word, I hate all the gods' – is her own declaration, her own slogan against all heavenly and earthly gods who do not recognise human self-consciousness as the highest divinity"[18] – but here it is the workers who are expected to challenge the Olympian deities of capitalism. The intended effects of such references rest on their breaking down the boundaries between past and present, in demonstrating, or perhaps more accurately asserting, unexpected continuities in institutions or ideas:

> Citizen Weston illustrated his theory for you by saying that, if a bowl contains a specific quantity of soup to feed a specific number of persons, an increase in the broadness of the spoon does not produce any increase in the amount of soup. He must allow me to find this illustration truly ladled out (*ausgelöffelt*). It reminded me somewhat of the simile in which Menenius Agrippa took refuge. When the Roman plebeians went on strike against the Roman patricians, the patrician Agrippa told them that the patrician belly provided the proletarian limbs of the body of the state with nourishment. Agrippa failed to show how someone could feed the limbs of one man by filling the belly of another. Citizen Weston, on his part, has forgotten that the bowl from which the workmen eat is filled with the whole product of the national labour, and that if one thing prevents the workers from taking more out of the bowl it is neither the narrowness of the bowl not the scantiness of its contents, but purely and simply the smallness of their spoons.[19]

Marx was by no means alone in his fondness for classical references. Despite their apparent irrelevance to the subject matter, writers on modern economic and social development continually threw in classical allusions, for rhetorical effect or simply because the dominance of classics in their early education made this a natural form of expression. Examples can be cited from Adam Smith's passing reference to "the Daedalian wings of paper money" – an effective critique of contemporary economic policy only if it could be assumed that all readers would identify the allusion to the fate of Icarus – to Max Weber's comments on the "Maecenases" of modern politics.[20] Ferdinand Tönnies took it for granted that his readers could read Latin – "supposing that life is conceived under that form of reality to which thinking itself belongs [*quatenus sub attributo cogitationis concipitur*]" – and recognize classical literary allusions: "the old saying of Seneca's: Velle non dixitur."[21]

> The scholar and scientist will be happy and content with the opinion he has of himself and in the knowledge of the depth and meaning of his insight (which is expressed in the famous line *Felix qui potuit rerum cognoscere causas*).[22]

Predictably, perhaps, given his background as an ancient historian and his self-proclamation as "the Thucydides of political economy," Wilhelm Roscher offered a cornucopia of ancient examples and references: numerous citations of Aristotle, of course, but also Martial on the cost of fresh water at Ravenna; Xenophon, Plato, and Cicero on ideas of wealth; Herodotus, Hippocrates, Euripides, Plutarch, and Strabo on the influence of climate; Xenophon and Cicero on price; and Xenophon and Plato on money.[23] This might be understandable, given Roscher's methodological assumption that economics needed to be understood in terms of its historical dimension. However, he appears to revert to the perspective of the political economy of a century before in his citation of sources like Cicero, Sallust, Appian, and Seneca to underpin assertions about the link between materialism and social decay, and is distinctly Marxian in his assertion that "Demosthenes *Phil*. IV, 144 cautions us against the Manchester criterion of national prosperity."[24] One might question how far such citations were likely to represent an effective rhetorical tactic, given the general tendencies of economic writing by this period – but they certainly mark out Roscher's work as distinctive, and may be seen as a deliberate attempt at making it more readable and accessible than the dry theories and tables of Ricardo and his followers. Economics, for Roscher, was not to be a narrow specialism, isolated from all external influences and read only by other specialists; it should display its awareness of the wider world of culture, and thereby, perhaps, also demonstrate the relevance of its ideas to the world beyond economics.

Classical allusions can represent a claim to authority – in the case of the economists, a claim to authority beyond their specialized field, or at least a means of emphasizing the breadth of their knowledge and experience beyond it. There is always the possibility that such references represent no more than what Matthew Arnold identified as the use of classical culture as a badge of educational background or cultural attainment:

> The culture which is supposed to plume itself on a smattering of Greek and Latin is a culture which is begotten by nothing so intellectual as curiosity; it is valued either out of sheer vanity and ignorance, or else as an engine of social and class distinction, separating its holder, like a badge or title, from other people who have not got it.[25]

Of course, it was always possible to claim that one's opponent was a dilettante, scattering classical allusions for the sake of it, while one's own references were essential for the development of the substantive argument.

Slavery, Ancient and Modern

To consider every separate allusion on its own merits – to review Marx's deployment of Greek tragedy or Roscher's fondness for Xenophon – would not only be a long and highly speculative exercise, but would undoubtedly place much greater weight and importance on throwaway comments than many of them could adequately bear. The importance of the theme of ancient slavery, however, can scarcely be disputed, and so it offers a useful case study for the different ways in which writers deployed ancient material and engaged with the idea of antiquity.

Slavery was, as has already been seen, a key theme in the confrontation of antiquity and modernity, often taken as one of the defining characteristics of the former and as the basis for a fundamental distinction between past and present in economic terms. "The chief difference between the domestic oeconomy of the ancients and that of the moderns consists in the practice of slavery," David Hume had argued.[26] According to Adam Smith, "there can, it seems, be little doubt that the scanty progress which ancient civilisation made in mechanical science . . . is to be explained by the prevalence of slavery."[27] Slavery is the reason, for Marx, why Aristotle was unable to grasp the true nature of the value of commodities:

> Greek society was founded on slave-labour, hence had as its natural basis the inequality of men and of their labour-powers. The secret of the

expression of value, the equality and equivalence of all kinds of labour, because and in so far as they are human labour in general, can only be deciphered when the concept of human equality already possesses the steadfastness of a popular prejudice.[28]

"Ancient civilization was either based directly on slavery or else was permeated by slavery to a degree never present in the European Middle Ages," noted Weber, offering this as the prime evidence for the absence of anything resembling the modern proletariat in antiquity, and the absence of guilds or other associations of free workers.[29]

Slavery's importance as a defining difference between past and present was not confined to the economic sphere. In Hegel's scheme of world-historical development, slavery represents the fundamental limitation of classical society:

> Among the Greeks the consciousness of freedom first developed, and as a result they became free; but they, like the Romans, knew only that some men were free, not that the human as such was. Even Plato and Aristotle did not know this. Therefore not only did the Greeks have slaves, and their life and the existence of their beautiful freedom was bound up with this, but their freedom was itself in part only an accidental, transient and limited blossoming and in part at the same time a hard servitude of the human and the humane.[30]

For John Stuart Mill, the abolition of slavery represented modernity's strongest claim to have surpassed antiquity.

> In political and social organization, the moderns, or some of them at least, have a more unqualified superiority over the Greeks. They have succeeded in making free institutions possible in large territories; and they have learnt to live and be prosperous without slaves. The importance of these discoveries – for discoveries they were – hardly admits of being over-rated. For want of the first, Greece lost her freedom, her virtue and her very existence as a people; and slavery was the greatest blot in her institutions while she existed.[31]

All of this might seem to raise questions about the integrity and value of classical civilization; certainly it suggests an obvious reason why nineteenth-century ancient historians, unlike economic or political commentators, largely steered clear of the subject of slavery or played down its significance.[32] The abolition of the evils of slavery offered clear grounds for modern triumphalism at antiquity's expense; surprisingly, however, many of these writers seemed more concerned to rescue antiquity from the worst implications of the accusation. This is precisely Mill's approach: "Even on the subject of slavery there are many, and not inconsiderable palliations."[33] Greek slavery was not based on race, and manumitted slaves could mix on equal terms with the community; it was relatively easy for them to escape, which must have been a check on ill usage; "the literature of the Athenians proves that they not only cultivated, but counted on finding, moral virtues in their slaves, which is not consistent with the worst form of slavery"; slavery did not lead to a disdain for manual labor. All of these statements are, considering the surviving historical evidence, arguable at best, and verging on special pleading. Far from being tainted by slavery, the Greek cultural achievement is brought forward by Mill both as evidence that their slavery must have been less severe than that of other societies and as mitigation for the fact that the Greeks had slaves at all – stressing that this was true of all ancient nations: "If with them, as in all antiquity, slavery existed as an institution, they were not the less the originators of political freedom, and the grand exemplars and sources of it to modern Europe."[34]

It was possible, indeed, to go further in arguing that Greek culture was to some extent a justification of slavery at that point in human development. Mill wavered on the edge of this argument:

> Doubtless, however, in Greece as elsewhere, slavery was an odious institution; and its inherent evils are in no way lessened by the admission, that as a temporary fact, in an early and rude stage of the arts of life, it may have been, nevertheless, a great accelerator of progress . . . The error was not so great of first introducing it, as of continuing it too long.[35]

Friedrich Engels chose to take a still longer view, emphasizing the place of Greece in the eventual rise of modernity:

> Without slavery, no Greek state, no Greek art and science; without slavery, no Roman Empire. But without the basis laid by Hellenism and the Roman Empire, also no modern Europe. We should never forget that our whole economic, political and intellectual development presupposes a state of things in which slavery was as necessary as it was universally recognised. In this sense we are entitled to say: without the slavery of antiquity, no modern socialism.[36]

Earlier writers had gone even further, emphasizing that the differences between ancient and modern society might make it inappropriate to judge slavery in modern terms. "To make mankind labour beyond their wants," argued Steuart, "to make one part of a state work to maintain the other gratuitously, could only be brought about by slavery, and slavery was therefore introduced universally. Slavery was then as necessary towards multiplication, as it would now be destructive of it."[37]

> The best for each epoch is that which suits it best . . . Institutions good at one period may be and most frequently are bad at another and *vice versa*. For example, slavery, which is now a monstrosity, was certainly at its origin an admirable institution, designed to prevent the strong from destroying the weak, constituting an unavoidable transition in the general development of civilisation.[38]

The issue of ancient slavery raised important questions about the existence of universal principles, the judgment of other historical periods, and the relative valuation of culture and justice. It represented a key point for debate, a permanently controversial issue that could be counted upon to create discomfort about the value placed on classical culture and on the dependence of modern society on the foundations laid by the Greeks. The power of the idea and its associations therefore represented valuable ammunition if the debate was turned away from antiquity and the emotions associated with slavery were introduced into the consideration of modernity.

In the first place, it was possible to undermine modernity's assumption of superiority by questioning the extent to which slavery had actually now been abolished. Rousseau had evoked this idea to suggest that modern economic practices were incompatible with liberty – "Give money, and soon you will have chains. The word *finance* is a slave's word; it is unknown in the City"[39] – and also declared that "you care more for your gain that for your freedom, and you fear slavery less than you fear poverty."[40] This approach was echoed by Wagner, who fully acknowledged the implications of slavery for the value of classical culture: "the slave, by sheer reason of the assumed necessity of his slavery, has exposed the null and fleeting nature of all the strength and beauty of exclusive Grecian manhood."[41] However, the subsequent development of human society, in Wagner's view, has not brought any improvement: "it has dragged down the fair, free man to itself, to slavery; the slave has not become a free man but the free man a slave."[42] The "slave of industry" exemplifies the condition of someone who labors merely for money and has no real love for his work; "his energy can never rise above the character of the busy strokes of a machine; in his eyes it is but weariness and bitter, sorrowful toil."[43] "The only man who feels free today, at least in the sense of freedom from open slavery, is he who has money; for he is thus able to employ his life to some other end than that of winning the bare means of subsistence."[44] The hollowness of modern claims to support freedom and culture is exposed; in fact, little has changed since antiquity, with even fewer positive results from this degradation of humanity than had been achieved in classical Greece.

Nietzsche was similarly skeptical that full human development could be possible within modern society, or that payment is sufficient to justify degradation.

> Poor, happy and independent – these things can go together; poor, happy and a slave – these things can also go together, and I can think of no better news I could give to our factory slaves: provided, that is, they do not feel it to be in general a *disgrace* to be thus used, and *used up*, as a part of a machine and as it were a stopgap to fill a hole in human inventiveness. To the devil with the belief that higher payment could lift from them the *essence* of their miserable condition – I mean their impersonal enslavement! To the devil with the idea of being persuaded that an enhancement of this impersonality within the mechanical operation of a new society could transform the disgrace of slavery into a virtue! To the devil with setting a price on oneself in exchange for which one ceases to be a person and becomes a part of a machine![45]

Wagner and Nietzsche, and especially the latter, tend towards the idea that there is something degrading in any form of manual labor – which was of course the attitude of many of the Greek philosophical sources. It was to be expected that Marx would take a different view, given his belief that productive activity was at the heart of human existence, but he was even more enthusiastic in invoking slavery as a means of characterizing the conditions of capitalism.

> "If," dreamed Aristotle, the greatest thinker of antiquity, "if every tool, when summoned, or even of its own accord, could do its appropriate work, just as the creations of Daedalus moved of their own accord, or the tripods of Hephaestus went through their own initiative to their sacred work, if the weavers' shuttles were thus to weave of themselves, then there would be

no need either of assistants for the master workers or of slaves for the lords." And Antipatros, a Greek poet of the time of Cicero, greeted the invention of the water-wheel for grinding corn, this elementary form of all product-ive machinery, as the liberator of the slave women and the restorer of the golden age! "Oh! those heathens!" They understood, as the learned Bastiat has discovered, and before him the still cleverer McCulloch, nothing of Political Economy and Christianity. They did not understand, for example, that the machine is the best-proven means of lengthening the working day. They excused to some extent the slavery of one man as a means to the full human development of another. But to preach slavery of the masses, in order to make some crude or half-educated parvenus into "eminent spinners," "extensive sausage-makers" and "influential shoe-black dealers," for that they lacked the specifically Christian quality.[46]

This is a complex passage, drawing together many of the themes in Marx's critique of modernity. It emphasizes the paradoxical and counter-intuitive nature of modernity, that labor-saving machinery should not save labor from any of its burdens; it contrasts ancient values with modern ones, as paganism is shown to value human beings in practice whereas Christianity claims to do so but actually contributes to their oppression; it offers an ironic dismissal of the unworthy ends for which this exploita-tion of human beings is being conducted, again in contrast to the ancient pursuit of full human development.[47] Above all, Marx offers the equation of modern factory labor with slavery – but slavery on an incomparably greater scale, and slavery which conceals the true nature of the relation between the modern "slave" and his master.

> They are not only slaves (*Knechte*) of the bourgeois class and of the bourgeois state, they are daily and hourly subjugated by the machine, by the observer, and above all by the individual bourgeois manufacturer himself.[48]

> From the social standpoint the working-class, even when it stands outside the unmediated labour process, is just as much an appendage of capital as the dead instruments of labour . . . Individual consumption ensures, on the one hand, the means for the workers' maintenance and reproduction and on the other hand, by the constant annihilation of the means of sub-sistence, their continual re-appearance on the labour-market. The Roman slave was bound by chains, the wage-labourer is bound to his owner through invisible threads. The appearance of his independence is maintained through the constant change in the identity of the individual employer and the *fictio iuris* of a contract.[49]

The modern worker appears to be free because he has the right to leave his job – but he cannot escape the necessity of labor within the capitalist system without starving. He appears to be free because he appears to be paid for his labor, rather than it being extracted from him by force, but this too is an illusion, according to Marx's theory of how the capitalist is able to profit from the employment of wage labor:

> Although only a part of the day's work of the worker is *paid*, the other part being *unpaid* labour, and precisely this unpaid or surplus labour constitutes the fund out of which surplus-value or profit is formed, it has the appearance as if the whole of the work is paid labour. This deceptive appearance is the distinguishing feature of wage-labour compared with other historical forms of labour. With the slave, even the *paid* part of his work appears to be unpaid.[50]

The rhetorical effect is first to undermine the contrast between ancient and modern and then to reverse it. Slavery is an evil, even when it enables the glorious development of Greek culture; however, it is an evil which modernity has failed to eradicate, whatever the opinions of its advocates and despite the potential within the modern economy for doing so – indeed, modernity has made slavery even more pervasive and pernicious. "All that modern nations have achieved is to disguise slavery at home and import it openly into the New World."[51] The modern laborer is more of a slave than the ancient slave because he believes that he is free and is properly rewarded for his work. It could easily be argued that modern factory labor is in fact nothing like slavery according to most definitions, but that is clearly beside the point: the powerful effect of Marx's account depends not on an explicit argument but on the unsettling of assumptions and the arousal of complicated emotions, revealing that all our outrage has been directed at the wrong target. Antiquity has been condemned; North America continues to be reproached; we should in fact turn our anger on our rulers, our society, and ourselves.

These deployments of the image of slavery take for granted that it is reprehensible; they seek simply to undermine the idea that modernity has done away with it, as a means of establishing the desperate need for a full revolutionary transformation of modern society that will abolish slavery in reality. Both Marx and Wagner look optimistically to the possibilities of technology as an emancipatory force, once a right relation is established between man and machinery:

When the brotherhood of man has cast this care for ever from it, and, as the Greeks upon their slaves, has lain it on machines – the artificial slaves of free creative man, whom he has served till now as the fetish worshipper serves the idol his own hands have made – then will man's whole enfranchised energy proclaim itself as nothing but pure artistic impulse. Thus shall we regain, in vastly higher measure, the Greek element of life.[52]

An alternative approach was to draw on the arguments about whether human slavery might, in a specific historical context, have been excusable or acceptable, in order to question more generally whether slavery might in fact be defensible. This was not necessarily intended as a serious proposition. James Steuart, for example, employed it as a means of undermining arguments denouncing "luxury" in the name of ancient ideals of frugality and virtue:

> If the simplicity of the ancients be worthy of imitation, or if it appear preferable to the present system, which it is not my business to decide, then either slavery must be introduced to make those subsist who do not labour, or they must be fed upon charity. Labour and industry can never, I think, be recommended on the one hand, and the effects of them proscribed on the other.[53]

In a similar manner, Rousseau sought in this way to question modern society's willingness to set limits on justice in the name of freedom and its claim that in so doing it had shown its superiority to the slave-owning Greeks:

> What? Freedom can only be maintained with the help of servitude? Perhaps. The two extremes meet. Everything that is not in nature has its inconveniences, and civil society more than all the rest. In some unfortunate circumstances one can preserve one's own freedom only at the expense of someone else's . . . As for you, modern peoples, you have no slaves, but are yourselves slaves; you pay for their freedom with your own. Well may you boast of this preference; I find it more cowardice than humanity.[54]

This is close to one of the key themes in Nietzsche's early work: the dependence of culture on slavery – expressed in the full conviction that this is fully justified as the means for the full development of the few – and the bad faith of modernity in trying to deny this. As he argued in *The Birth of Tragedy*, the Alexandrian culture needs a slave-class in order to be able to exist in the long term; however, it denies, in its optimistic view of existence, that such a class is necessary, and so, when the effect of its beautiful words of seduction and pacification about "human dignity" and "dignity of labour" is exhausted, it goes gradually towards a dreadful annihilation.[55]

In his essay on "The Greek State," these ideas are developed at greater length, constantly evoking a contrast with the Greeks in terms both of cultural achievement and of honesty:

> We moderns have an advantage over the Greeks in two ideas, which are given as something like a consolation to a world behaving thoroughly slavishly and yet fearfully avoiding the word "slave": we talk of the "dignity of man" and of the "dignity of labour." Everybody torments himself in order to perpetuate miserably a miserable existence; this awful necessity compels him to consuming labour, which now the man – or, more accurately, the human intellect – seduced by the "will" from time to time admires as something dignified. So that labour may have a claim to an honourable title, it would be above all necessary that existence itself, to which labour is only a painful means, should have more dignity and value than until now it seems to have had for serious philosophies and religions . . .
>
> In the modern world . . . the greed of the struggle for existence and the need for art often show themselves in the same man at the same time: out of which unnatural amalgamation has developed the requirement to excuse and to consecrate that first greed in preference to this need for art. Therefore we believe in the "dignity of man" and the "dignity of labour."
>
> The Greeks did not require such conceptual hallucinations, for among them it is said with shocking frankness that labour is a disgrace . . . Labour is a disgrace, because existence has no value in itself; even if this existence gleams in the seductive jewellery of artistic illusions and now really appears to have a value in itself, the statement that labour is a disgrace is still valid – indeed precisely because of the feeling that it is impossible for the man fighting for more continuing existence to be an *artist*. In the modern period it is not the art-needing man who determines the general conceptions, but the slave, who by his nature must describe all his relationships with deceptive names in order to be able to live.[56]

This argument represents an absolute and self-conscious rejection of the Marxian idea of humanity, and of all attempts at bringing equality and freedom to the mass of society; in Nietzsche's scheme these are simply slavish values, just as Christianity is the morality of the slave.[57] Modernity is either lying or deluded in claiming that freedom is the birthright of all men; that is possible only at the expense of art, the only thing that makes life worth living. Rather than trying to excuse or explain away the fact that the Greeks kept slaves and yet produced great art, let alone seeking to condemn them for it or question the value of their art, we must face the full implications of the connection between these two facts.

> We must agree to accept this cruel-sounding truth, that *slavery is an intrinsic part of culture*; a truth of course which leaves no doubt as to the absolute value of existence. *This* is the vulture that gnaws at the liver of the Promethean promoter of culture. The misery of arduously-living men must yet increase, in order to make possible the production of the world of art possible to a small number of Olympian men.[58]

> Every moment devours the preceding one, every birth is the death of innumerable beings, begetting, living and murdering are all one. Therefore we may compare this splendid culture with a blood-stained victor, who in his triumphal procession carries the defeated along chained to his chariot as slaves, whom a beneficent power has blinded so that, almost crushed by the wheels of the chariot, they still cry "Dignity of labour!" "Dignity of man!" The voluptuous Cleopatra-culture tosses again and again the most priceless pearls into her golden cup; these pearls are the tears of sympathy with the slaves and their misery. The enormous social crisis of the present has been born out of the mollycoddling of modern man, not out of the true and deep compassion for that misery; and if it should be true that the Greeks perished on account of their having slaves, then another fact is much more certain, that we shall perish through the *lack* of slavery.[59]

Past and Present

> The fact is that civilization requires slaves. The Greeks were quite right there. Unless there are slaves to do the ugly, horrible, uninteresting work, culture and contemplation become almost impossible. Human slavery is wrong, insecure and demoralizing. On mechanical slavery, on the slavery of the machine, the future of the world depends.
>
> Oscar Wilde, *Soul of Man*, 141

Oscar Wilde here attempts something resembling a compromise between the positions of Marx and Nietzsche, which is likely to satisfy neither of them: his approach continues to devalue labor as the basic activity of human existence, and it persists in the naively optimistic view that science will enable all human beings to be free and cultured. In political terms, but also in terms of the way that past and present are related to one another, Wilde's argument is clearly much closer to that of Marx; on the essential issue of the condition of the majority of its inhabitants, modernity differs from antiquity only in appearance, and a revolution in society is necessary in order to abolish slavery in reality as well as in name. For Nietzsche, modernity is absolutely distinct from antiquity – and that is the root of its cultural decay.

These perspectives clearly demonstrate the ways in which antiquity could be used both to diagnose the ailments of modernity, by analyzing the nature of the differences between past and present, and to denounce it by drawing upon the accumulated reverence for classical culture and the society that produced it. They also show how divergent the conclusions drawn from such a confrontation of past and present might be. Philologically and historically, Nietzsche's account of antiquity is perfectly reasonable, not only in his recognition of the dependence of Greek culture on slavery but also in his account of Greek philosophical attitudes towards labor; it is a self-avowedly elitist and aristocratic vision, so that debates on the incidence of slaveholding in the lower ranks of Athenian society are beside the point. Marx says little directly about ancient slavery, and so seems less vulnerable to philological criticism, but from a Nietzschean perspective one might identify some evasions, subterfuges, or simply loose phraseology: his failure to make a direct connection between slavery and culture (rather, as seen in the passage in the *Grundrisse*, the Greek cultural achievement is linked to the limited development of technology, conventionally but here not explicitly explained by slavery); the rhetorical contrast between the chained Roman slave and the modern worker (when in fact most ancient slaves were not chained but acquiesced, for whatever reason, in their own exploitation); the very partial account of Aristotle's theory of slavery (neglecting to mention his belief in the existence of "slaves by nature").

The most glaring incompatibilities between the two perspectives become clear when they bring the past into closer relation with the present. Each could, on the basis of their own philosophical, political, and moral premises, develop an extensive critique of the other: Marx's naïve scientific optimism and slavish *ressentiment* against aristocratic values versus Nietzsche's cruel, inhuman, and essentially egotistical wish to revert to the childish world of antiquity.[60] The difficulty lies in developing any alternative criteria for evaluating these accounts that would not be open to similar political and psychological critique. We cannot choose between their diagnoses of modernity or their suggested remedies except on pre-conceived political or moral grounds; however, we can attempt to eval-uate other aspects. Each is primarily rhetorical rather than philosophical, intended to force a confrontation with modernity and to inspire dissat-isfaction with the present state of society; it is verging on tautology to suggest that Marx's approach has a more obvious appeal to a broader audi-ence whereas Nietzsche's extreme vision is confined to a tiny number of like-minded elitists, since those are exactly the audiences that each of them seeks to address. The passages operate at different levels of irony, with different purposes in mind; certainly Marx is sincerely committed to the cause of liberating the workers from their current condition, whereas Nietzsche is less concerned with offering a genuine remedy for the ills of modernity than, through his usual weapons of paradox and hyperbole, forcing it to confront its own bad faith and self-deception.[61] Nietzsche's style and approach seem intended to force the reader into a decision, either for or against true culture, for or against the rights of man, in full know-ledge of what he sees as the implications of this choice.[62]

Marx and Nietzsche have a similar vision of the purpose of studying antiquity. Each had a love of classical art and literature and of the idea of antiquity for their own sake, but in both cases this is subordinated to the need to analyze and confront modernity; ideas, including or especi-ally ideas about antiquity, are never an end in themselves, but should always be brought into a relation with the present. Both writers exemplify the idea of Hegel that "it is necessary that we appropriate the world of antiquity not only to possess it, but ever more to digest and transform it."[63] Each would claim, doubtless, to be appropriating antiquity in order to further its spirit: Marx, in order to overthrow the alienating, anti-human aspects of modernity and thus recreate Greek culture and community at a higher level, and Nietzsche, in order to undermine the naïve human-istic understanding of the world and human nature that claims to find support for its ideals in the classical past.

The comments of Marx and Nietzsche, and especially their accounts of ancient slavery, emphasize the disputed nature of such concepts as "an-tiquity" and "modernity," "classical" and "modern," so that the dialectic of modernity as not-classical and antiquity as not-modern yields widely divergent, and frequently wholly incompatible, interpretations, diagnoses, and remedies. However, their works also exemplify the power of the idea of antiquity as a means of estranging oneself (and one's readers) from the present and so promoting the development of a new understanding and critical spirit – and, perhaps above all, the power of the idea that there needs to be an alternative, a touchstone, something other than modernity, to which we can refer in making sense of our own situation.

> Philology as a science of antiquity naturally does not last for ever, its subject matter can be exhausted. What cannot be exhausted is the ever-new adaptation of an age to antiquity, the comparison of the two. If one sets the philologist the task of better understanding *his* time by means of antiquity, his task will be never-ending. This is the antimony of philology: one has always actually understood *antiquity* only by means of the *present* – and shall the present now be understood by means of antiquity?[64]

Notes

1 See e.g. Martindale (1993); Martindale and Thomas (2006).
2 Cf. Fleming (2006).
3 Porter (2000a) and (2000b).
4 *Vorlesungen über die Philosophie der Geschichte*, 22.
5 Ibid., 88.
6 "On classical studies," 328.
7 *Wir Philologen*, 109.
8 Ibid., 104.
9 *Die Geburt der Tragödie*, 130.
10 *Daybreak*, 195.
11 "Study of economic history," quoted in Collini, Winch, and Burrow (1983), 272.
12 See generally McCarthy (1992).
13 *Kapital*, I, 430; McCarthy (1994), 3–65.
14 *Kapital*, I, 74.
15 McCarthy (1990).
16 *Kapital*, I, 441, 924–5.
17 *Kapital*, I, 675.
18 *Differenz der demokritischen und epikureischen Naturphilosophie*, 262. The line is quoted in Greek.
19 Marx, *Lohn, Preis und Profit*, 106.
20 Smith, *Wealth of Nations*, II.ii.86; Weber, "Politics as a vocation," 103.
21 *Community and Society*, 103, 144.
22 *Community and Society*, 128, quoting – but not referencing – Vergil, *Georgics*, 2.490.
23 *Principles of Political Economy*, I, e.g. 53 n.8, 55 n.4, 62 n.4, 136 n.5, 307 n.9, 342–3 n.5, 350 n.10.

24 Ibid., 100–1.
25 *Culture and Anarchy*, 43.
26 "On the populousness of antient nations," 385.
27 *Wealth of Nations*, IV.ix.47.
28 *Kapital*, I, 74.
29 *Agrarian Sociology of Ancient Civilizations*, 42; *The City*, 201.
30 *Vorlesungen über die Philosophie der Geschichte*, 31.
31 "Grote's History of Greece II," 314.
32 Finley (1980).
33 "Grote's History of Greece II," 315.
34 "Grote's History of Greece I," 273.
35 "Grote's History of Greece II," 315.
36 *Anti-Dühring*, 168.
37 *Inquiry into the Principles of Political Oeconomy*, I, 50.
38 Comte, "Plan of the scientific operations," 153.
39 *Of the Social Contract*, III.15.2.
40 Ibid., III.15.9–10.
41 *Art and Revolution*, 50.
42 Ibid.
43 Ibid., 49.
44 Ibid., 51.
45 Nietzsche, *Daybreak*, no. 206.
46 Marx, *Kapital*, I, 430–1.
47 McCarthy (1994), 50–61.
48 Marx and Engels, *Manifest der Kommunistischen Partei*, 469.
49 Marx, *Kapital*, I, 598–9.
50 *Lohn, Preis und Profit*, 134.
51 Letter from Marx to P. V. Annenkov, December 28, 1846.
52 Wagner, *Art and Revolution*, 57.
53 *Inquiry into the Principles of Political Oeconomy*, I, 123.
54 *Of the Social Contract*, III.15.10.
55 *Die Geburt der Tragödie*, 117.
56 "Die griechische Staat," 764–5.
57 Nehemas (1985) 109–12; Staten (1990), 40–60; Solomon (1996), 208–11.
58 Nietzsche, "Die griechische Staat," 767.
59 Ibid., 768–9.
60 Cf. generally Love (1986).
61 Cf. Porter (2000b), 145–7, 208.
62 On Nietzsche's style, see Nehemas (1985), 13–41; Solomon (1996), 185–6.
63 "On classical studies," 327.
64 Nietzsche, *Wir Philologen*, 107.

Bibliography of Sources

† Published posthumously (works by Hegel marked † were compiled from a mixture of his lecture notes and those of people who heard him).

Arnold, M., *Culture and Anarchy* [1869], ed. J. D. Wilson, Cambridge (1932).

Baudelaire, C., "The painter of modern life" [1863], in *The Painter of Modern Life and Other Essays*, ed. and trans. J. Mayne, London (2nd edn., 1995).

Bücher, K., *Entstehung der Volkwirtschaft* [1893], trans. S. M. Wickett as *Industrial Evolution*, New York (1968).

Bury, J. B., *A History of Greece to the Death of Alexander the Great*, 2 vols., London (1902).

Coleridge, S. T., *A Course of Lectures* [1818], in *Complete Works*, IV, New York (1853).

Comte, A., "Philosophical considerations on the sciences and savants" [1825], in *The Crisis of Industrial Civilization: The early essays of Auguste Comte*, trans. H. D. Hutton, London (1973).

Comte, A., "Plan of the scientific operations necessary for reorganizing society" [1822], in *The Crisis of Industrial Civilization: The early essays of Auguste Comte*, trans. H. D. Hutton, London (1973).

Comte, A., *Positive Philosophy* [1830], trans. H. Martineau, 2 vols., 2nd edn., London (1875).

Constant, B., "De la liberté des anciens comparée à celle des modernes" [1819], in *La liberté chez les modernes: écrits politiques*, ed. M. Gauchet, Paris (1980).

Durkheim, E., *The Division of Labour in Society* [1893], trans. G. Simpson, Glencoe and London (1933).

Durkheim, E., "The dualism of human nature and its consequences" [1914], in *On Morality and Society: Selected writings*, ed. and trans. R. N. Bellah, Chicago (1973).

Durkheim, E., "Montesquieu and Rousseau" [1892], in *On Morality and Society: Selected writings*, ed. and trans. R. N. Bellah, Chicago (1973).

Durkheim, E., Review in *L'Année Sociologique* [1906], in *Selected Writings*, ed. A. Giddens, Cambridge (1972): 60–3.

Engels, F., *Anti-Dühring* [1877], in K. Marx and F. Engels, *Collected Works*, 25, London (1987).

Freud, S., *Introductory Lectures on Psychoanalysis* [1916–17], trans. J. Strachey, London (1963).

Goethe, J. W. von, "Winckelmann" [1805], trans. H. B. Nisbet, in H. B. Nisbet, ed., *German Aesthetic and Literary Criticism*, Cambridge (1985).

Gramsci, A., *Prison Notebooks* [1929–35], trans. J. A. Buttigieg, 2 vols., New York (1996).

Hegel, G. W. F., *Aesthetics: Lectures on fine art* [†1835], trans. T. M. Knox, Oxford (1975).

Hegel, G. W. F., *Elements of the Philosophy of Right* [1821], trans. T. M. Knox, Oxford (1952).

Hegel, G. W. F., "The German Constitution" [1798–1802], in *Political Writings*, ed. L. Dickey and H. B. Nisbet, trans. H. B. Nisbet, Cambridge (1999).

Hegel, G. W. F., *Lectures on the Philosophy of Religion* [†1832], ed. P. C. Hobson, trans. R. F. Brown *et al.*, Berkeley, CA (1985).

Hegel, G. W. F., "On classical studies" [1809], in *Early Theological Writings*, trans. T. M. Knox, Oxford (1948).

Hegel, G. W. F., *Phenomenology of Spirit* [1807], trans. A. V. Miller, Oxford (1977).

Hegel, G. W. F., *Vorlesungen über die Philosophie der Geschichte* [†1840], in *Werke*, 12, Frankfurt (1970).

Herder, J. G. von, *On the Cognition and Sensation of the Human Soul* [1778], in *Philosophical Writings*, ed. and trans. M. N. Forster, Cambridge (2002).

Herder, J. G. von, *This Too a Philosophy* [1774], in *Philosophical Writings*, trans. and ed. M. N. Forster, Cambridge (2002).

Humboldt, W. von, *The Sphere and Duties of Government* [1852], trans. J. Coulthard, 1854; reprinted Bristol (1996).

Hume, D., *Enquiries Concerning Human Understanding and the Principle of Morals* [1748], ed. L. A. Selby-Bigge, 2nd edn., Oxford (1902).

Hume, David, "Of commerce" [1742], in *Essays: Moral, political and literary*, I, ed. T. H. Green and T. H. Grose, London (1882).

Hume, David, "Of refinement in the arts" (Originally entitled "Of luxury") [1742], in *Essays: Moral, political and literary*, I, ed. T. H. Green and T. H. Grose, London (1882).

Hume, David, "On the populousness of antient nations" [1742], in *Essays: Moral, political and literary*, I, ed. T. H. Green and T. H. Grose, London (1882).

Kant, I., "Conjectures on the beginning of human history" [1786], in *Political Writings*, ed. H. Reiss, trans. H. B. Nisbet, 2nd edn., Cambridge (1991).

Kant, I., "Idea for a universal history with a cosmopolitan purpose" [1784], in *Political Writings*, ed. H. Reiss, trans. H. B. Nisbet, 2nd edn., Cambridge (1991).

Kierkegaard, S., *The Sickness Unto Death: A Christian psychological exposition for upbuilding and awakening* [1849], in *Kierkegaard's Writing*, XIX, ed. and trans. H. V. and E. H. Hong, Princeton, NJ (1980).

Kierkegaard, S., *Two Ages: The age of revolution and the present age: A literary review* [1845], in *Kierkegaard's Writing*, XIV, ed. and trans. H. V. and E. H. Hong, Princeton, NJ (1978).

List, F., *The National System of Political Economy* [1841], trans. S. S. Lloyd, London (1904).

Malthus, T. R., *An Essay on the Principle of Population* [2nd edn., 1803], London (1973).

Malthus, T. R., *Principles of Political Economy* [2nd edn., 1836], London (1936).

Mann, T., "Reflections of an unpolitical man" [1918], in *Gesammelte Werke*, XII, Frankfurt (1974).

Marshall, A., *Principles of Economics: An introductory volume* [1890], 8th edn., London (1920).

Marx, K., *Die achtzehnte Brumaire des Louis Bonaparte* [1852], in *Marx–Engels Werke*, 8, Berlin (1960).

Marx, K., *A Contribution to the Critique of Political Economy* [1859], in K. Marx and F. Engels, *Collected Works*, XXIX, London (1987).

Marx, K., *Differenz der demokritischen und epikureischen Naturphilosophie* [1841], in *Marx–Engels Werke*, 1, Berlin (1974).

Marx, K., *Economic and Philosophical Manuscripts of 1844* [1844], in K. Marx and F. Engels, *Collected Works*, III, London (1975).

Marx, K., *The German Ideology* [1845–6], in K. Marx and F. Engels, *Collected Works*, V, London (1976).

Marx, K., *Grundrisse* [1857–8], trans. M. Nicolaus, Harmondsworth (1973).

Marx, K., *Kapital*, Volume I [1867], in *Marx–Engels Werke*, 23, Berlin (1962).

Marx, K., *Kapital*, Volume III [†1894], in *Marx–Engels Werke*, 25, Berlin (1983). Marx, K., *Lohn, Preis und Profit* [1865], in *Marx–Engels Werke*, 16, Berlin (1964).

Marx, K., *The Poverty of Philosophy* [1847], in K. Marx and F. Engels, *Collected Works*, VI, London (1976).

Marx, K., *Results of the Immediate Process of Production* [1863–6], trans. B. Fowkes, included in Marx, *Capital: A critique of political economy*, I, Harmondsworth (1976).

Marx, K., Speech at the Anniversary of the *People's Paper* [1856], in K. Marx and F. Engels, *Collected Works*, XIV, London (1980).

Marx, K. and Engels, F., *Manifest der Kommunistischen Partei* [1848], in *Marx–Engels Werke*, 4, Berlin (1964): 459–93.

Mill, J. S. "Civilization" [1836], in *Collected Works*, XXVII, ed. J. M. Robson, Toronto (1977).

Mill, J. S., "Grote's History of Greece I" [1846], in *Collected Works*, XXIV, ed. A. M. and J. M. Robson, Toronto (1986).

Mill, J. S., "Grote's History of Greece II" [1847], in *Collected Works*, XXIV, ed. A. M. and J. M. Robson, Toronto (1986).

Mill, J. S., "On liberty" [1859], in *Collected Works*, XVIII, ed. J. M. Robson, Toronto (1977).

Mill, J. S., *Principles of Political Economy* [1848], 7th edn., London (1871).

Mill, J. S., "Sedgwick's Discourse" [1835], in *Collected Works*, X, ed. J. M. Robson, Toronto (1969).

Mommsen, T., *The History of Rome* [1854], 4 vols., 2nd edn., London (1864–6).

Nietzsche, Friedrich, *Beyond Good and Evil* [1885], trans. R. J. Hollingdale, Cambridge (1990).

Nietzsche, Friedrich, *Daybreak* [1881], trans. R. J. Hollingdale, Cambridge (1982).

Nietzsche, Friedrich, *Die Geburt der Tragödie* [1872], in *Sämtliche Werke: Kritischen Studienausgabe*, I, ed. G. Colli and M. Montinari, Berlin (1967–77): 23–156.

Nietzsche, Friedrich, *Götzen-Dämmerung oder Wie man mit dem Hammer philosophirt* [1889], in *Sämtliche Werke: Kritische Studienausgabe*, VI, ed. G. Colli and M. Montinari, Berlin (1967–77): 55–161.

Nietzsche, Friedrich, "Der griechische Staat" [1872], in *Sämtliche Werke: Kritischen Studienausgabe*, I, ed. G. Colli and M. Montinari, Berlin (1967–77): 764–77.

Nietzsche, Friedrich, "Homer's Wettkampf" [1872], in *Sämtliche Werke: Kritischen Studienausgabe*, I, ed. G. Colli and M. Montinari, Berlin (1967–77): 783–92.

Nietzsche, Friedrich, "Die Philosophie im tragischen Zeitalter der Griechen" [1873], in *Sämtliche Werke: Kritischen Studienausgabe*, I, ed. G. Colli and M. Montinari, Berlin (1967–77): 801–72.

Nietzsche, Friedrich, "Über Wahrheit und Lüge im aussermoralischen Sinne" [1873], in *Sämtliche Werke: Kritischen Studienausgabe*, I, ed. G. Colli and M. Montinari, Berlin (1967–77): 875–90.

Nietzsche, Friedrich, *Unzeitgemässe David Strauss der Bekenner und der Schriftsteller Betrachtungen*, I [1873], in *Sämtliche Werke: Kritischen Studienausgabe*, I, ed. G. Colli and M. Montinari, Berlin (1967–77): 159–242.

Nietzsche, Friedrich, *Vom Nutzen und Nachtheil der Historie für das Leben: Unzeitgemässe Betrachtungen*, II [1874], in *Sämtliche Werke: Kritischen Studienausgabe*, I, ed. G. Colli and M. Montinari, Berlin (1967–77): 245–334.

Nietzsche, Friedrich, *Wir Philologen* [unpublished notes, 1875], in *Werke*, IV.1, ed. G. Colli and M. Montinari, Berlin (1967).

Quincey, T. de, *Logic of Political Economy* [1842–3], in *The Works of Thomas de Quincey*, XIV, ed. J. Whale, London (2001).

Ricardo, D., *Works and Correspondence*, VII: Letters, 1816–18, ed. P. Sraffa, Cambridge (1952).

Roscher, W., *Principles of Political Economy* [1854], trans. J. J. Lalor, 2 vols., Chicago (1878).

Rousseau, J.-J., *Discourse on the Origin and Foundations of Inequality (Second Discourse)* [1755], in *The Discourses and Other Early Political Writings*, ed. and trans. V. Gourevitch, Cambridge (1997).

Rousseau, J.-J., *Discourse on Political Economy* [1755], in *The Social Contract and Other Later Political Writings*, ed. and trans. V. Gourevitch, Cambridge (1997).

Rousseau, J.-J., *Discourse on the Sciences and Arts (First Discourse)* [1750], in *The Discourses and Other Early Political Writings*, ed. and trans. V. Gourevitch, Cambridge (1997).

Rousseau, J.-J., "Last reply" [1753], in *The Discourses and Other Early Political Writings*, ed. and trans. V. Gourevitch, Cambridge (1997).

Rousseau, J.-J., *Of the Social Contract* [1762], in *The Social Contract and Other Later Political Writings*, ed. and trans. V. Gourevitch, Cambridge (1997).

Saint-Simon, C.-H. de Rouvroy, Comte de, "Of the industrial system" [1821], in *The Political Thought of Saint-Simon*, ed. and trans. G. Ionescu, Oxford (1976).

Saint-Simon, C.-H. de Rouvroy, Comte de, "Of social organisation" [†1825], in *The Political Thought of Saint-Simon*, ed. and trans. G. Ionescu, Oxford (1976).

Say, J.-B., Article for the *Décade Philosophique* [1796], in *An Economist in Troubled Times*, ed. and trans. R. R. Palmer, Princeton, NJ (1997).

Say, J.-B., "Lecture at the Collège de France" [1832], in *An Economist in Troubled Times*, ed. and trans. R. R. Palmer, Princeton, NJ (1997).

Say, J.-B., "On the influence of the future progress of economic knowledge on the fate of nations" [1828], in *An Economist in Troubled Times*, ed. and trans. R. R. Palmer, Princeton, NJ (1997).

Say, J.-B., *A Treatise on Political Economy* [1803], ed. C. C. Biddle, trans. C. R. Prinsep, New York (1971).

Schiller, F., *Gedichte 1776–1799: Schillers Werke Nationalausgabe*, I, ed. J. Petersen and F. Beissner, Weimar (1943).

Schiller, F., "On naïve and sentimental poetry" [1795–6], trans. J. A. Elias, in H. B. Nisbet, ed., *German Aesthetic and Literary Criticism*, Cambridge (1985).

Schiller, F., *Über die ästhetische Erziehung des Menschen* [1795], Stuttgart (1965).

Schlegel, A. W. von, *Lectures on Dramatic Art and Literature* [1809–11], in T. Webb, ed., *English Romantic Hellenism 1700–1824*, Manchester (1982).

Simmel, G., *Philosophy of Money* [1907], trans. T. Bottomore and D. Frisby, London (1978).

Simonde de Sismondi, J. C. L., *Nouveaux principes de l'économie politique* [1819], 2 vols., 2nd edn., Paris (1827).

Smith, A., *An Inquiry into the Nature and Causes of the Wealth of Nations* [1776], ed. R. H. Campbell and A. S. Skinner, 2 vols., Oxford (1976).

Spengler, O., *Der Untergang des Abendlandes* [1918], Munich (1980).

Steuart, J., *Inquiry into the Principles of Political Oeconomy* [1770], 2 vols., Edinburgh (1966).

Taylor, Thomas, *The Mystical Initiations; or Hymns of Orpheus* [1787], in T. Webb, ed., *English Romantic Hellenism 1700–1824*, Manchester (1982).

Tönnies, F., *Community and Society* [1887], ed. and trans. C. P. Loomis, New York (1963).

Toynbee, A., *Lectures on the Industrial Revolution of the Eighteenth Century in England* [1884], 3rd edn., London (1908).

Wagner, R., "Art and climate" [1850], in *The Art-Work of the Future and Other Works*, trans. W. A. Ellis, London (1895).

Wagner, R., *Art and Revolution* [1849], in *The Art-Work of the Future and Other Works: Prose Works* I, trans. W. A. Ellis, London (1895).

Wagner, R., *The Art-Work of the Future* [1849], in *The Art-Work of the Future and Other Works*, trans. W. A. Ellis, London (1895).

Wallace, R., *A Dissertation on the Numbers of Mankind in Antient and Modern Times*, Edinburgh ([1753]).

Weber, M., *The Agrarian Sociology of Ancient Civilizations* [1909], trans. R. I. Frank, London and New York (1988).

Weber, M., *The City* [†1920], trans. D. Martindale and G. Neuwirth, New York (1958).

Weber, M., *Economy and Society* [†1921; 4th edn., 1956], ed. G. Roth and C. Wittich, New York (1968).

Weber, M., "Politics as a vocation" [1918–19], in *From Max Weber: Essays in Sociology*, ed. and trans. H. H. Gerth and C. Wright Mills, London (1948).

Weber, M., *The Protestant Ethic and the Spirit of Capitalism* [1904–5], trans. Talcott Parsons, reprinted London (1992).

Weber, M., "The Protestant sects and the spirit of capitalism" [†1920–1], in *From Max Weber: Essays in Sociology*, ed. and trans. H. H. Gerth and C. Wright Mills, London (1948).

Weber, M., "Religious rejections of the world and their directions" [1915], in *From Max Weber: Essays in Sociology*, ed. and trans. H. H. Gerth and C. Wright Mills, London (1948).

Weber, M., "Science as a vocation" [1918–19], in *From Max Weber: Essays in Sociology*, ed. and trans. H. H. Gerth and C. Wright Mills, London (1948).

Weber, M., "The social causes of the decline of ancient civilization" [1896], trans. R. I. Frank, in *The Agrarian Sociology of Ancient Civilizations*, London and New York (1988).

Wilde, O., "The soul of man under socialism" [1891], in *The Soul of Man Under Socialism and Selected Critical Prose*, ed. L. Dowling, London (2001).

Winckelmann, J. J., *History of the Art of Antiquity* [1764], trans. H. F. Mallgrave, Los Angeles, CA (2006).

Winckelmann, J. J., "Thoughts on the imitation of the painting and sculpture of the Greeks" [1755], trans. H. B. Nisbet, in H. B. Nisbet, ed., *German Aesthetic and Literary Criticism*, Cambridge (1985).

Zweig, S., *Die Welt von Gestern: Erinnerungen eines Europäers* [1939–41], Frankfurt (1970).

Bibliography

Beiser, F. C., ed. (1993) *The Cambridge Companion to Hegel*, Cambridge.

Bauman, Z. (2000) *Liquid Modernity*, Cambridge.

Berman, M. (1982) *All That Is Solid Melts Into Air: The experience of modernity*, New York.

Berry, C. J. (1994) *The Idea of Luxury: A conceptual and historical investigation*, Cambridge.

Bottomore, T. (1985) *Theories of Modern Capitalism*, London.

Brown, P. (1971) *The World of Late Antiquity*, London.

Callinicos, A. (1995) *Theories and Narratives: Reflections on the philosophy of history*, Cambridge.

Carandini, A. (1983) "Columella's vineyard and the rationality of the Roman economy," *Opus* 2: 177–204.

Cohen, G. A. (1978) *Karl Marx's Theory of History: A defence*, Oxford.

Coleman, D. C. (1987) *History and the Economic Past: An account of the rise and decline of economic history in Britain*, Oxford.

Coleman, D. C. (1992) *Myth, History and the Industrial Revolution*, London.

Collini, S., Winch, D. and Burrow, J. (1983), *That Noble Science of Politics: A study in nineteenth-century intellectual history*, Cambridge.

Davidson, A. (1977) *Antonio Gramsci: Towards an intellectual biography*, London and Atlantic Highlands, NJ.

Derrida, J. (1994) *Specters of Marx: The state of the debt, the work of mourning and the new international*, trans. P. Kampf, New York.

Dodge, C. H. (1980) *Benjamin Constant's Philosophy of Liberalism: A study in politics and religion*, Chapel Hill, NC.

Edwards, C., ed. (1999) *Roman Presences: Receptions of Rome in European culture, 1789–1945*, Cambridge.

Entwhistle, H. (1979) *Antonio Gramsci: Conservative schooling for radical politics*, London, Boston, MA, and Henley.

Finley, M. I. (1979) *The Bücher–Meyer Controversy*, New York.

Finley, M. I. (1980) *Ancient Slavery and Modern Ideology*, London.

Finley, M. I. (1985) *The Ancient Economy*, 2nd edn., London.

Fleming, K. (2006) "The use and abuse of antiquity: The politics and morality of appropriation," in Martindale and Thomas (2006): 127–37.

Gay, P. (1970) *The Enlightenment: An interpretation*, 2: *The science of freedom*, London.

Geuss, R. (2005) "Thucydides, Nietzsche and Williams," in *Outside Ethics*, Princeton, NJ: 219–33.

Giddens, A. (1990) *The Consequences of Modernity*, Cambridge.

Goldhill, S. (2002) *Who Needs Greek?: Contests in the cultural history of Hellenism*, Cambridge.

Gooch, G. P. (1920), *History and Historians in the Nineteenth Century*, 2nd edn., London.

Goody, J. (2004) *Capitalism and Modernity: The great debate*, Cambridge.

Gossman, L. (2000) *Basel in the Age of Burckhardt: A study in unseasonable ideas*, Chicago and London.

Grimmer-Solem, E. (2003) *The Rise of Historical Economics and Social Reform in Germany, 1864–1894*, Oxford.

Habermas, J. (1987) *The Philosophical Discourse of Modernity*, trans. F. Laurence, Cambridge.

Hall, S., Held, D., Hubert, D., and Thompson, K., eds. (1995) *Modernity: An introduction to modern societies*, Cambridge.

Hamilton, P. (1996) *Historicism*, London and New York.

Harvey, D. (1989) *The Condition of Postmodernity*, Oxford.

Heller, A. (1999) *A Theory of Modernity*, Oxford.

Hennis, W. (1988) *Max Weber: Essays in reconstruction*, trans. K. Tribe, London.

Hingley, R. (2000) *Roman Officers and English Gentlemen: The imperial origins of Roman archaeology*, London and New York.

Hodgson, G. M. (2001) *How Economics Forgot History: The problem of historical specificity in social science*, London and New York.

Houlgate, S. (1991) *Freedom, Truth and History: An introduction to Hegel's Philosophy*, London.

Humphreys, S. C. (1978) *Anthropology and the Greeks*, London.

Kadish, A. (1989) *Historians, Economists and Economic History*, London.

Kain, P. J. (1982) *Schiller, Hegel, and Marx: State, society, and the aesthetic ideal of ancient Greece*, Kingston and Montreal.

Käsler, D. (1988) *Max Weber: An introduction to his life and work*, trans. P. Hurd, Cambridge.

Koselleck, R. (2004) *Futures Past: On the semantics of historical time*, trans. K. Tribe, New York.

Krieger, L. (1977) *Ranke: The meaning of history*, Chicago and London.

Latour, B. (1993) *We Have Never Been Modern*, trans. C. Porter, Hemel Hempstead, Hertfordshire.

Loraux, N. (1996) "Back to the Greeks? Chronique d'une expédition lointaine en terre connue," in J. Revel and N. Wachtel, eds., *Une École Pour les Sciences Sociales*, Paris: 275–97.

Love, J. R. (1991) *Antiquity and Capitalism: Max Weber and the sociological foundations of Roman civilization*, London.

Love, N. S. (1986) *Marx, Nietzsche and Modernity*, New York.

Luce, T. J. and Woodman, A. J., eds. (1993) *Tacitus and the Tacitean Tradition*, Princeton, NJ.

Magnus, B. and Higgins, K. M., eds. (1996) *The Cambridge Companion to Nietzsche*, Cambridge.

Marchand, S. L. (1996) *Down from Olympus: Archaeology and philhellenism in Germany, 1750–1970*, Princeton, NJ.

Martindale, C. (1993) *Redeeming the Text: Latin poetry and the hermeneutics of reception*, Cambridge.

Martindale, C. (2006) "Introduction: Thinking through reception," in Martindale and Thomas (2006): 1–13.

Martindale, C. and Thomas, R., eds. (2006) *Classics and the Uses of Reception*, Oxford.

McCarney, J. (2000) *Hegel on History*, London and New York.

McCarthy, G. E. (1990) *Marx and the Ancients: Classical ethics, social justice, and nineteenth-century political economy*, Savage, MD.

McCarthy, G. E. (1994) *Dialectics and Decadence: Echoes of antiquity in Marx and Nietzsche*, Savage, MD.

McCarthy, G. E. (2003) *Classical Horizons: The origins of sociology in ancient Greece*, New York.

McCarthy, G. E., ed. (1992) *Marx and Aristotle: Nineteenth-century German social theory and classical antiquity*, Savage, MA.

Meikle, S. (1995) *Aristotle's Economic Thought*, Oxford.

Meinecke, F. (1972) *Historism: The rise of a new historical outlook*, trans. J. E. Anderson, London.

Meyer, E. (1922) *Kleine Scriften zur Geschichtstheorie und zur wirtschaftsliche und politischen Geschichte des Altertums*, Halle.

Mitzman, A. (1973) *Sociology and Estrangement: Three sociologists of imperial Germany*, New York.

Momigliano, A. (1990) *The Classical Foundations of Modern Historiography*, Berkeley, CA.

Morley, N. (1998) "Political economy and classical antiquity," *Journal of the History of Ideas* 26: 95–114.

Morley, N. (2004a) *Theories, Models and Concepts in Ancient History*, New York and London.

Morley, N. (2004b) "Decadence as a theory of history," *New Literary History* 35.4: 573–85.

Morley, N. (2004c) "Unhistorical Greeks: Myth, history and the uses of antiquity," in P. Bishop, ed., *Nietzsche and Antiquity: His reaction and response to the classical tradition*, Rochester, NY and Woodbridge, Suffolk.

Müller, R. (1972) "Hegel und Marx über die antike Kultur," *Philologus* 118: 1–31.

Nehemas, A. (1985) *Nietzsche: Life as literature*, Cambridge, MA.

Nelson, E. (2004) *The Greek Tradition in Republican Thought*, Cambridge.

Nippel, W., ed. (1993) *Über das Studium der Alten Geschichte*, Munich.

Outram, D. (1995) *The Enlightenment*, Cambridge.

Pearson, H. W. (1957) "The secular debate on economic primitivism," in K. Polanyi, C. M. Arensberg, and H. W. Pearson, eds., *Trade and Markets in the Early Empires: Economies in history and theory*, New York and London: 3–11.

Polanyi, K. (1944) *The Great Transformation: The political and economic origins of our time*, New York.

Porter, J. I. (2000a) *Nietzsche and the Philology of the Future*, Stanford, CA.

Porter, J. I. (2000b) *The Invention of Dionysus: An essay on The Birth of Tragedy*, Stanford, CA.

Potts, A. (1994) *Flesh and the Ideal: Winckelmann and the origins of art history*, New Haven, CT and London.

Punter, D. (1980) *The Literature of Terror: A history of Gothic fiction from 1765 to the present day*, London.

Reill, P. H. (1975) *The German Enlightenment and the Rise of Historicism*, London.

Riley, P., ed. (2001) *The Cambridge Companion to Rousseau*, Cambridge.

Roberts, J. T. (1994) *Athens on Trial: The antidemocratic tradition in Western thought*, Princeton, NJ.

Rosen, S. (1989) *The Ancients and the Moderns: Rethinking modernity*, New Haven, CT and London.

Rostovtzeff, M. I. (1926) *A History of the Ancient World*, I: The Orient and Greece, trans. J. D. Duff, Oxford.

Sannwald, R. (1957) *Marx und die Antike*, Zurich.

Scaff, L. A. (1989) *Fleeing the Iron Cage: Culture, politics and modernity in the thought of Max Weber*, Berkeley, Los Angeles, CA and London.

Sekora, J. (1977) *Luxury: The concept in western thought, Eden to Smollett*, Baltimore, MD.

Shaw, B. D. (1992) "Under Russian eyes," *Journal of Roman Studies* 82: 216–28.

Shklar, J. N. (2001) "Rousseau's images of authority," in Riley (2001): 154–92.

Skinner, A. S. (1975) "Adam Smith: An economic interpretation of history," in A. S. Skinner and T. Wilson, eds., *Essays on Adam Smith*, Oxford: 154–78.

Solomon, R. C. (1996) "Nietzsche *ad hominem*: Perspectivism, personality, and *ressentiment* revisted," in Magnus and Higgins (1996): 180–222.

Staten, H. (1990) *Nietzsche's Voice*, Ithaca, NY and London.

Stray, C. (1998) *Classics Transformed: Schools, universities and society in England, 1830–1960*, Oxford.

Strong, T. B. (2000) *Friedrich Nietzsche and the Politics of Transfiguration*, Urbana IL.

Trevelyan, H. (1981) *Goethe and the Greeks*, Cambridge.

Voltaire, *Philosophical Dictionary* [1764], trans. T. Besterman, Harmondsworth (1972).

Williams, R. (1983) *Keywords: A vocabulary of culture and society*, London.

Winch, D. (1996) *Riches and Poverty: An intellectual history of political economy in Britain, 1750–1834*, Cambridge.

Wokler, R. (2001) "Ancient postmodernism in the philosophy of Rousseau," in Riley (2001): 418–43.

Wolfreys, J. (2001) *Victorian Hauntings: Spectrality, Gothic, the uncanny, and literature*, Basingstoke, Hampshire.

Wood, E. M. (1995) *Democracy Against Capitalism: Renewing historical materialism*, Cambridge.

Wrigley, E. A. (1987) "The classical economists and the industrial revolution," in *People, Cities and Wealth: The transformation of traditional society*, London: 21–45.

Yack, B. (1992) *The Longing for Total Revolution: Philosophic sources of social discontent from Rousseau to Marx and Nietzsche*, Berkeley, CA, Los Angeles, CA, and London.

Index of Persons

Index of Subjects